Rainmakers: Born or Brea
Second edition

BY PATRICIA K. GILLETTE
WITH CONTRIBUTIONS FROM REBECCA HARDING

Commissioning editor
Alex Davies

Managing director
Sian O'Neill

Rainmakers: Born or Bred, second edition
is published by

Globe Law and Business Ltd
3 Mylor Close
Horsell
Woking
Surrey GU21 4DD
United Kingdom
Tel: +44 20 3745 4770
www.globelawandbusiness.com

Rainmakers: Born or Bred, second edition

ISBN 978-1-78742-925-3
EPUB ISBN 978-1-78742-926-0
Adobe PDF ISBN 978-1-78742-927-7

Contents

Executive summary

Rainmakers: Born or Bred, second edition is about changing the business development conversation and focusing on how remote working has impacted the way business opportunities can be cultivated and developed. Unlike other approaches to business development, this book uses actual data from practicing lawyers, gathered by the highly acclaimed Rainmaker Study, to highlight the personal characteristics that are common in successful rainmakers – and what holds others back from achieving their true potential. While acknowledging the negative associations many lawyers have with the "S" word – selling – this book encourages lawyers to embrace the reality that this is exactly what business development is and in doing so redefines and refocuses the traditional approach to business development.

It explores the benefits to stepping out of the safety net of simply being a great lawyer – which is vital in today's competitive market – noting that successful rainmakers have great reputations plus something else: they know how to build relationships by truly engaging with clients, understanding their business needs and challenges, and putting the interests of the client front and center. It is these two "Rs" – Reputation and Relationships – that are the keys to building sustainable, rewarding client relationships.

This second edition of *Rainmakers: Born or Bred* helps you access and enhance the characteristics that make rainmakers successful and provides you with practical ideas to implement immediately as you set out on your journey to improve your business development skills. Fully updated with an in-depth focus on digital and social media, this book is packed with opinions and advice from actual clients and rainmakers alike. It will help you make the most of the business development opportunities that present themselves every day – while staying true to your own personality.

Chapter one considers the common opinion that lawyers are fundamentally different from "non-lawyers" – that is, everyone else. This attitude artificially elevates the legal profession above that of other professions, and therefore above the clients for whom we work. It has been used to justify the position that "selling" is beneath our profession, should be done by someone else, or is simply not necessary. In chapter two we propose that, in the modern legal market, this is a view that very few of us can afford to have. So, how do we develop business without feeling as though we are "selling out"?

Chapter three answers that question by introducing the two "Rs" that make a successful rainmaker – the ability to build reputations and relationships, whilst exploring the techniques and behaviors that will allow you to effectively build your reputation and visibility, both within your firm and externally.

In chapter four we rely on data gathered from lawyers across the country in the original Rainmaking Study to identify the personal characteristics that make a successful rainmaker, and how these characteristics can be used to help us build relationships with internal and external clients alike. The next four chapters consider how these characteristics – Engagement, Dominance, Motivation, and Risk-taking – can act as a framework on which to build our own skills and strengths, to become more effective rainmakers.

The same listening skills that are so effective in formal pitches can also be applied to everyday interactions and chapter five equips the reader with practical steps to make the most of these engagement opportunities. Dominance – that is, the ability to communicate our advice in a manner that persuades others and engenders trust – is covered in chapter six. This skill requires us to understand the business context in which our advice is given, to tailor it accordingly, and to deliver it in a way that is oriented toward business solutions for our clients. Motivation is the focus of chapter seven. While we know that the skills and techniques of rainmaking can be leveraged by any lawyer to build stronger relationships, serve clients better, and win more work, rainmakers motivate others by delegating responsibility and empowering team members. Rainmakers also treat their clients as an integral part of their team. Building on what we have learned about dominance and motivation, chapter eight highlights the importance of taking risks, a characteristic that is critical to a rainmaker's success. Here, we outline ways in which we can improve our risk tolerance level so that we can turn perceived risks into constructive opportunities.

With the characteristics identified and the strategies for enhancing and building upon those characteristics laid out, chapter nine then looks at the various sources of business that are available, from existing clients to industry-specific networking opportunities.

Chapter ten, written by Rebecca Harding, brings the skills of the rainmaker into the modern age by introducing the inevitability of digital media, and what it means for business development.

Finally, chapter 11 captures practical advice from actual clients who hire lawyers every day. Their comments are filled with valuable information that confirms the importance of building reputation as well as relationships. These insights provide further information that will be helpful to you as you develop and hone your business development skills.

About the authors

Patricia K. Gillette is one of the leading experts and most sought-after speakers on gender diversity and equality. Rated as a top employment litigator and trial lawyer by *Chambers* and other organizations for 40 years and as a leader and rainmaker in her firms, Patricia's legal career focused on solving the most critical business issues of Fortune 500 clients. At the end of 2015, she resigned from her firm to pursue her passion for empowering women through keynote speaking and writing.

She was also invited to join the Judicial Arbitration and Mediation Services organization in San Francisco and has become one of the most popular mediators for employment cases.

Patricia is a frequent speaker in the United States and abroad at conferences, retreats, and professional association meetings. The bestselling first edition of *Rainmakers: Born or Bred* was widely acclaimed for the practical tactics and strategies she identifies that can be easily implemented to enhance business development skills and books of business.

Patricia has been widely recognized for her work to advance women in the profession. Most recently, she was chosen as the 2018 recipient of the ABA Margaret Brent Award, the highest honor given to women lawyers for professional achievements and advancing the interests of women lawyers. She has also received the ABA Golden Hammer Award, the California Women Lawyers Association's Fay Stender Award, the Transformational Leadership Award as one of the Top Women Rainmakers, and the Barristers Association of San Francisco Award of Merit.

Patricia is the co-founder of the Opt-In Project, a nationwide initiative focused on changing the structure of law firms to increase the retention and advancement of women. Her team at the 2016 Diversity Lab Hackathon created the Mansfield Rule, requiring that 30 percent of all candidates for leadership positions be women or minorities. The Mansfield Rule has been adopted by over 60 firms nationwide and is increasing the visibility and pipeline of women and minorities for leadership positions in firms and organizations.

Patricia has been a commissioner on the ABA Commission on Women in the Profession, a member of ABA's Gender Equity Task Force, co-chair of the BASF No Glass Ceiling Initiative, and she has served on several non-profit boards dedicated to protecting and promoting women and girls, including Equal Rights Advocates, Girls Leadership, Legal Momentum, and DirectWomen.

Rebecca Harding is a communications, marketing, and business development specialist. She is the worldwide chairman of the Society of Women Writers and Journalists, and was recently awarded Highly Commended Finalist in the UK Institute of Directors' Non-executive Director of the Year award. She is a professional member of the Chartered Institute of Public Relations and is a retired vice chairman of the Chartered Institute of Marketing. Rebecca founded Saltwhistle Communications in 2000 and has developed a portfolio of clients within the professional services industry. Clients range from multinational firms such as accountants Deloitte, PwC, and EY to law firms such as Stephenson Harwood, Norton Rose Fulbright, and Weightmans, as well as international businesses such as WPP's Mediacom, J Walter Thompson (now Wunderman Thompson), and Mindshare. Each client benefits from a range of services, including partner and board advisory services, digital and classic communications and marketing solutions, pitching and business development, and courses for professionals. Much of Rebecca's current work is international and she works with firms to increase their international effectiveness, as well as helping to draw together their international tenders/pitches. Prior to establishing Saltwhistle Communications, Rebecca was responsible for communications at Andersens. She also worked in marketing within the energy industry, with corporations such as BNFL, BP, ESSO, and Shell.

Introduction

What makes someone a successful rainmaker? That is what I was wondering one day as I was listening to yet another lecture about business development. And, as usual, the lecture focused on what I would describe as the "tactics" of business development – building a reputation and having a "plan". I thought to myself, if business development were this easy, then why isn't everyone a rainmaker? – because any competent attorney can develop a reputation and have a plan for bringing in business.

As a successful rainmaker in my 40 years of practicing law, I suspected there was more to the equation. In fact, I knew the dirty little secret of rainmaking and business development, which is this: business development is just a fancy, lawyer-like way of saying "selling". And selling requires more than just a good reputation. That particular "S" word, however, is one that lawyers don't like to embrace or acknowledge because it seems inconsistent with our lofty profession.

And yet, selling is exactly what we do when we engage in business development: we sell ourselves, our firms, our reputations, and our expertise. Once you accept that premise, the whole approach to business development changes. Why? Because we know that the most successful salespeople are those who are not only selling an excellent product (in legal terms, that would be your reputation and expertise) but who also know how to establish relationships so that clients want to "buy" the product. And it is building the relationship part of business development skills that law schools and law firms have ignored for years. We don't teach it, we don't talk about it, and many of us don't know how to do it.

"Successful rainmakers care deeply – perhaps unusually so – about personal relationships. Some rainmakers focus on relationships as a means to control how, on what and with whom they work. Others simply derive deep satisfaction from helping others. But all successful rainmakers strive for lasting and meaningful personal relationships."

Mitchell Zuklie, chairman, Orrick, Herrington & Sutcliffe LLP

That is what this book is all about. It is about changing the business development conversation. It is about changing the way we train people, the way we interact with our clients, the way we think about how we bring clients into our firms. It is about a new construct that recognizes the power and value of relationships as we sell our legal expertise. It is about making it rain!

Chapter 1:

Business development – who needs it?

Law schools have done a disservice to their students by making them think that being a successful lawyer is only about being an excellent lawyer.

Law firms have then perpetuated this myth by hiring new attorneys based on their pedigree, thus continuing the traditional notion that the lawyers who will be the most successful in their firms are those individuals who went to a few elite law schools, were on law review, and, perhaps, even clerked for a judge.

Is this wrong? Not completely. But it is wrong-headed because, for most firms, being a really smart lawyer isn't enough to make you successful in the competitive market of law firms. The reason for this is simple. Law firms are businesses, and that means they must make money. Money comes from clients choosing one firm of really smart lawyers over another firm of really smart lawyers.

So, the truth is that firms must have lawyers who can not only do excellent work but who can also bring in new clients and keep them. The skills required to accomplish that are not necessarily synonymous with having only a remarkable pedigree. But the fact is that you can be the smartest person in the room, from the best law school in the country with accolades galore, but if you can't relate to your clients, if you can't communicate your ideas in a way that mere mortals can understand, all that knowledge and expertise will be for naught – because clients won't want to work with you. Your relationships become your differential in the marketplace – your unique selling point.

Make your relationships your differential

This does not seem like an earth-shattering concept. But it does force us, as lawyers, to think about ourselves and our profession in a different way. Traditionally, we have considered ourselves above the fray. We are different from all other professions. That is why we call anyone who is not a lawyer a "non". Yes, we call them non-lawyers. Think about that. There is no such thing as a non-CEO, a non-accountant, or a non-physician. But, in our world, everyone who isn't an attorney is called and thought of as a "non".

Because we think of the world in this way, we sometimes forget that it is the non-lawyers, the businesspeople, whose business we are trying to bring into our firms (and I include in-house lawyers as businesspeople, because they quickly learn from their business clients that if they try to live in the lawyer/non-lawyer paradigm they will not be successful). And businesspeople will judge you against their other advisors. If you are too elevated as a lawyer, they will turn elsewhere to build practical, close business relationships.

In fact, if you ask a businessperson what makes an excellent lawyer, the answer you will get is broader than simply where the person went to law school.

> *"Transitioning from outside counsel to in-house requires a fundamental shift from clean-up crew to party planner. In-house lawyers get into the facts early – ideally before there is a significant legal issue. They are expected to play a greater role in the decisions being made, and, at times, wear many hats. In addition to being able to clearly articulate the legal risks to non-lawyers, in-house lawyers need to provide a menu of business savvy options, outline real-world consequences that might flow from each one, and then influence the client to make the best decision considering all factors – legal and non-legal. On any given day, I play the role of a lawyer, salesman, journalist, clairvoyant and psychologist. Having outside counsel that understands this complicated landscape, who can offer more than just the straightforward legal analysis, is invaluable."*
>
> Heidi Swartz, associate general counsel,
> labor and employment, Facebook

Because many lawyers graduate from law school without understanding this fundamental fact – that being smart and clever about the law is not enough – it is up to firms to drive this point home and train their lawyers not only on how to be great at their craft but also on how to sell their product through all the means and channels that are available to them. At the end of the day, those lawyers who have good reputations for excellent legal work and who know how to build relationships with non-lawyers, both in person and online, are actually the most valuable assets to their firms.

Chapter 2:
Getting comfortable with the "S" word

S is for selling

The "S" word – selling – is not something lawyers like to talk about. In fact, for many in our profession, anything connected with "sales" conjures up images of infomercials and the QVC channel. And yet, when we are courting new clients we are selling our firms, our teams, our expertise, our experience, and our judgment. That is our product. Just like the person who sells a computer, a car, or a phone, we are selling our ability to use our legal expertise and training to help clients realize their business goals, while minimizing the legal risks.

There certainly are some lawyers who are able to bring in business simply because of their amazing legal skills. But those are the exceptions, not the rule. In fact, many of those lawyers had an unusual opportunity that allowed them to build a reputation that is larger than life and, as a result, business comes to them based solely on their reputation and their results.

But, for the vast majority of lawyers, having a good reputation is not enough. If you are like most of us, you need something more. You need to develop the personal characteristics that make clients want to work with you, because most rainmakers are lawyers who not only have great reputations but also know how to engage with people, how to persuade their clients in helping them make good business decisions, and how to motivate their clients and colleagues. They are risk takers for themselves and their clients. It is these "extras" that catapult an excellent lawyer into a successful rainmaker.

Here is how one rainmaker put it:

> *"Modestly speaking, I think people genuinely like talking to me. I am a really good listener but I also know how to keep a conversation going and make people feel comfortable. I think that makes people want to be around me and work with me."*
>
> Meryl Macklin, partner, Bryan Cave LLP

R is for reputation and relationships

So, in fact, there are two "Rs" that define most successful rainmakers: reputation and relationships. Building a reputation requires that you are an excellent lawyer in terms of how you think, write, analyze, and communicate. Building relationships requires that you know how to make people want to work with you, trust you, put their faith in you, and count on you to help them deliver on their business goals.

Being able to sell your product – that is, your skills as a lawyer – requires that you present yourself as someone who is knowledgeable, flexible, interesting, and interested. Because, after all, clients are just people. They want to work with someone who knows what they are doing – which is determined at the first pass by reputation. But they also want to work with someone who understands their business, who knows that their job is to help execute and realize the business strategy, who can speak in a language that businesspeople understand and can relate to, and who is innovative, creative, and strategic. Those are the skills you must "sell" once a client has asked you to bid for a case or a deal. These days, we can build the foundations of that reputation, and the perception of those skills, before meeting clients in person through our online connections. If the online content we create demonstrates that we have those attributes, we are halfway to winning the battle before that face-to-face meeting.

Some lawyers are natural salespeople, but most need some prodding to develop those skills and to get comfortable with them. That comes from making sure lawyers understand what it takes to become a successful rainmaker. Most firms focus business development training on building reputation by speaking and writing articles and then formulating a business plan with deliverables. There is no question that such tactics are necessary. But if firms want training programs that will truly arm their attorneys with the skills they need to be successful rainmakers, those programs must focus on developing the interpersonal skills that build relationships.

Heidi Friedman, a partner at Thompson Hine LLP, described the traits that led to her success as a rainmaker as follows:

> *"Emotional intelligence, hardworking, relatable; ability to listen, ability to take constructive criticism and hear someone say no; perseverance."*

Robert Stein, formerly of counsel at Coblentz Patch Duffy & Bass LLP, and rainmaker extraordinaire, uses different words but conveys the same concept:

> *"[Most clients want] to trust a lawyer's judgment, they want immediate access, they want cost efficiency and they want empathy."*

Finally, Catherine Arrowhead, a partner at Parker & Poe, says this:

> *"Treat your client's case as if it was yours or your family's problem. Manage outcome expectations, but always give it your all."*

Creating opportunities

But even with all the training firms provide and the advice of actual rainmakers, there are still some obstacles that we must recognize and firms must address if we are truly committed to leveling the playing field. One of those obstacles that adversely impacts women and people of color is implicit bias. This is an unspoken challenge for many law firms and it continues to plague our industry.

To address this problem, firms must put systems in place to ensure that women and diverse attorneys are getting the same chances as white males to access current and potential clients of the firm. This means monitoring pitch opportunities to ensure teams are diverse in terms of gender, sexual orientation, race, and ethnicity. It also means proactively choosing qualified women and diverse attorneys to work assignments that give them the exposure they need to be prepared to be first chairs at trials and lead persons on deals. And it means putting in place succession planning for institutional clients to include diverse attorneys, so that they can "inherit" those relationships that historically have been passed on to white male lawyers.

As you read on, you will come to understand from the Rainmaker Study that most women and diverse attorneys have or can develop the personal characteristics that will make them successful at bringing in business. But they can maximize those skills if they also have the same opportunities as their white male counterparts. That is why addressing systemic issues, like implicit bias, head on is so critical to moving the dial.

Chapter 3: The first "R" of business development

Business development requires focus on two "Rs" – reputation and relationships. All lawyers need to understand that there is no substitute for an excellent reputation. So, let's start there.

A reputation that will win and keep clients means demonstrated excellence in legal analysis, writing, communicating, and service to the client. The definition of "the client", however, evolves during your legal career, starting with your colleagues in your firm and then moving to the traditional notion of clients – companies and individuals outside of your firm.

Building a reputation in your first few years

Attorneys in law firms build their reputations initially by doing incredible work for the senior associates and partners for whom they work. Those are your initial "clients" as a new associate, and studies show that within weeks of your start date, your competence and abilities will be assessed and cemented in the minds of many with whom you work.

To build your reputation internally you must meet deadlines, provide value, answer the questions you are asked succinctly and coherently, and look for other ways to add value to the problem or issue you are evaluating. For example, if you were asked as a first-year associate what the statute of limitations is for filing a claim, you should, of course, answer that question. But you might consider going further: defining the circumstances in which the statute may be tolled or citing exceptions to the application of the statute. Showing that you can think beyond the issue presented to you indicates that you understand the role of an attorney is to think both broadly and specifically and to find creative solutions to problems presented by clients.

In the days before electronic documents, I remember an incident where a first-year associate was preparing the documents for an upcoming deposition. He gave them to me in a binder that was tabbed and had an index. He had ordered them by subject and then chronologically. I expected that. But he also put them in a box, with a yellow legal pad and several pencils, and sent them to my home. This may sound ridiculous, but what it said to me is that he recognized his job was to make my preparation as easy as possible, both in terms of substance and the practical matter of getting a deposition outline done – in those days by paper and pencil.

Another example that stands out is a new associate who missed a filing deadline. She acknowledged the mistake, and provided me – without being asked – several alternative ways to ask for relief from the missed deadline. And she didn't bill an hour of time for doing so. We were able to obtain relief for her error, and instead of thinking of this young woman as someone who had screwed up I thought of her as someone who was mature, responsible, and a problem solver.

> *"[I always did] excellent work... I was extremely responsive regardless of whether I was dealing with clients, partners, or senior associates. I came through on my promises. I tried to be creative, thoughtful and proactive."*
>
> Joan Haratani, partner, Morgan, Lewis & Bockius LLP

Reputation internally is also built by how you present yourself to your superiors and colleagues. You are a lawyer, so look like one and act like one. What does that mean? It means you should present yourself as a professional at work and at work-sponsored outside events. That goes for how you dress, how you talk, how you react to criticism, and how you relate to your colleagues. This also means that you volunteer for assignments that might be outside of your safety zone, you take on challenges, and you express an interest in the business of the firm and in your progression within the firm. You ask for opportunities to work on matters, to go on outings with clients and partners, and to be included in meetings and events with lawyers internally and externally. It means creating content for social media platforms for the firm, such as generating blogs and ideas for webinars and podcasts. You will enhance not only your own reputation through these, but those of your fellow professionals and your firm.

> *"First, I learned the law, which included writing articles for partners and tagging along at every opportunity, whether to a presentation, court appearance, client visit, etc. I tried to make it easy for the partners to bring me along by making it clear I would not bill for my time... Happy partners make an associate's life much better, and provide a great foundation to build one's own reputation."*
>
> Tim Long, shareholder, Greenberg Taurig LLP

So, kudos to the associate who asks a partner out to lunch to get to know him or her. High marks to the associate who hears about a project that is interesting and asks how he/she can help. Praise to the associate who raises his/her hand with an idea for a blog or speech on a new issue in his/her practice area. And, as Joan Haratani, partner at Morgan Lewis says, "*Identify those senior attorneys in your firm or company that you admire and ask them to mentor you*". These are things that make you stand out from the crowd and begin to build your reputation internally. These kinds of things involve risk-taking and networking skills.

Another critical part of building your reputation internally is asking for feedback after every significant project. That tells the person with whom you are working that you care about the value and quality of the work you have done. It also shows that you are looking to grow from each experience. And because most partners often don't take the time for (or try to avoid) giving feedback, you have to ask for it. That is not how it should be, but that is how it is in many firms. So, take the initiative and ask for information about your performance from the people with whom you work.

But, when you do ask for feedback, be prepared to accept what you are told. Don't expect praise, but accept it when it is given. Take criticism constructively and ask for opportunities to show improvement. This is especially important for first years who often feel crushed by criticism. Don't let that happen to you. Being a lawyer is a hard job. You worked hard to get here. Give yourself time to grow into the job, which means accepting both compliments and criticisms and always striving to do your best.

In your first years as an associate, you have to be careful about offering excuses for mistakes or criticisms from a partner or senior associate. Statements like, "I was trying to meet your deadline but I took so long drafting this, I just didn't have time to proofread" may be more damaging to your reputation than the typos you are trying to explain. As a partner, that makes me think that you didn't manage your time well or that you procrastinated, or that you simply weren't willing to go that extra step to finish the job professionally. That is not the message you want to convey.

On the other hand, there will be times when you think the senior person you are working with has leveled unjustified criticism toward you. Rather than responding on the spot, give it some time. Talk to a mentor about how to address it, consider how to best approach the senior person, and then do so in a manner and tone that is calibrated to the magnitude of the issue and the personality of the senior person.

Building your reputation as you advance in your career

While your first few years will be focused primarily on building your reputation with your immediate colleagues and members of your firm, by your third or fourth year you should be focusing your energy externally as well. The first rule of encounters with persons outside of the firm is this: treat everyone you meet as a potential client. You never know who will advance in an organization. So, whether you are working with a low-level businessperson or the head of litigation, you should treat everyone the same – with respect, deference, and humility. You may think you are more accomplished, smarter, or more savvy, but that doesn't matter. You are in a service industry and your job is to serve your clients.

Why is this important? Because many of the people who you meet at lower levels within their organizations, or even in other law firms, will advance into positions of power. One of my clients started out as an entry-level human resources person. I, at the time, was a new associate. We bonded over our career goals, our family situations, our professional interests, and our personal interests. As she progressed in her career she took me with her, as her outside counsel. She displaced other firms to bring me into each new company she went to; she fought the legal departments in her organizations to be able to use me, even with my firm's higher rates. Over her career and mine, the business she sent me generated millions of dollars for my firms.

The same is true of other lawyers with whom you work, even as a junior associate. They too can move into positions of power and a source of business:

> *"In the late 1980s, early 1990s, I worked on a big class action with lots of lawyers from around the country. One of them later went in-house at Sprint, and because she knew me well from the previous case, sent me the business."*
>
> Meryl Macklin, partner, Bryan Cave LLP

The advantage of the contacts you establish though your online platforms and social media is that they will stay with you as the years pass by. They may grow professionally, but you will maintain that digital contact and the relationship throughout.

Building your external reputation also requires that you find a way to differentiate yourself from other lawyers. That means you must think out of the box and show people outside of your firm that you are creative and strategic. Often you can do that by writing blogs or articles, or conducting webinars to groups of lawyers and groups of businesspeople. But writing or speaking on the "same old, same old" take on an issue or problem is not an effective use of your time. If you are going to invest time in any type of content, then find a different angle on the issue, a new way of approaching it, a creative way of describing or presenting it. You want to stand out; you want to be the one they remember. When you are presenting a speech, for example, think about a) whether to use a program such as PowerPoint; and b) how to use it. My advice? Use PowerPoint for emphasis, not content. The mistake so many people make is putting too much information on their PowerPoint slides. Then, instead of facing the audience when they present, they read from the screen, which is usually behind them. Or, the audience reads the screen and only half listens to the presentation. That impacts the value of your speech. If you use PowerPoint, bullet point the important concepts and use your interesting and effective presentation to explain the bullet points. If you want to offer more detail, write a paper as well and include that in the materials that accompany your presentation and, of course, prominently include your contact information.

Now the digital landscape makes it so much easier to gain exposure. As well as the opportunities presented by in-person events, you have a wealth of news platforms, digital trade journals, social media, and other outlets for your ideas and thinking. The trick is to ensure that the audiences you are reaching are the right ones for you. If you create content for one outlet you can repackage it and use it elsewhere. One idea can go a long way. For example, a blog can become a help sheet or a webinar, as well as social media posts. More on this in chapter ten.

When I was trying to build my reputation, I took any speaking engagement that came along. I would speak to the Rotary Club, the local merchants' associations, industry conferences, and bar association events. How did I get those gigs? I asked for them. I went to friends and family and made "cold calls" to organizations offering to be their lunchtime speaker on a topic that was relevant to their group.

At those events, I would do whatever it took to make my presentation memorable and relevant to the audience. For example, while other lawyers were explaining to these groups of businesspeople the esoteric reasons why one court's opinion on a certain issue was different from another court's opinion, I would talk about the top ten ways businesses could avoid litigation in employment cases. In that discussion, I might reference uncertainty within the courts on a certain point, but because I was talking to businesspeople, I didn't talk about the intricacies of those conflicts. Instead, I focused on the impact that uncertainty might have on choices they made regarding their employees. That resonated with these audiences; in-depth discussions of the law, for the most part, did not. But if I were speaking to a group of employment lawyers about new developments in the law, my presentation would be filled with "lawyer talk" – although I would find a way to make it interesting to keep with my goal of being the "creative and out-of-the-box" thinker. I used to be a frequent speaker at conferences that attracted high-level employment lawyers from across the country. I always made sure my presentations were different from other presenters. For example, I sometimes opened with a few phrases from a relevant song ("Take this job and shove it" when talking about constructive discharge cases; "Stand by your man" when talking about sexual harassment cases where consent appeared to be an issue). I may not have a great voice, but people remembered my speech. Just to be clear, however – I am not suggesting this as a tactic everyone (or anyone) should use. But it was consistent with my brand and my personality and to this day there are people who will say, "Oh yeah, you are the one who sings".

Peppering content with personal examples of cases or deals on which you have worked – particularly if you talk about things that distinguish you from other lawyers – also builds your reputation. Readers and listeners love to hear relevant war stories and if you can present those in a big-picture, succinct (be careful of giving too many details), engaging way to your audiences, they will remember you for the stories you have told. And that builds reputation.

For example, when talking about trial tactics I often relay a situation where I used an advertising agency, instead of trial consultants, to assist with trial themes and opening statements. That is an unusual approach and very different from what clients generally hear from lawyers. Some find it shocking; others find it amazing. But all of them remember it and so they remember me, and that builds my reputation as someone who thinks differently from most lawyers.

But remember; articles, webinars, and speaking engagements don't necessarily yield clients directly. They build reputation because your name begins to become a household word so, when asked about you, people say, "I have heard of her".

These kinds of activities are part of branding yourself and raising your visibility. It may be years before they yield a client. That doesn't mean you shouldn't do them, it just means you should be patient.

As Michelle Banks, former general counsel of the Gap Inc. and now senior advisor at Baker Gilmore, says:

"When I was a general counsel, I cannot think of a situation where we hired someone solely on the basis of an article they wrote. But we did consider, and in some instances engage, lawyers we heard speak at conferences. I would not dismiss writing articles, however, because they are opportunities to build your brand by showcasing your expertise, they may help you get a speaking engagement, and they are opportunities to remind people of you and your expertise."

As Michelle suggests, it is possible that something you say or do at an event or in an article will yield immediate results. The case on which I billed more fees than any other single case in my career came from a speech I gave at an employment law conference in which I talked about how I would handle a particular type of claim. The approach I suggested was quite unique, it caught the attention of one of the lawyers in a large legal department, and that led to meeting with the general counsel, where my firm was retained to handle the case.

Promoting yourself means just that – taking credit for achieving results. Don't waste those opportunities by being coy or self-deprecating. For example, there are two ways of reporting back from a difficult hearing:

"I was so nervous at the hearing. The judge was mean and asked really tough questions. I luckily had read a case he focused on the night before so I was able to respond to his questions, but my voice was shaking and I thought I was going to throw up. But, he finally ruled in our favor, thank God."

Or: *"I went to the hearing. We won."*

Which do you think is more effective with the partner who asked you to argue the motion?

Building your reputation externally and internally also requires self-promotion. This means you have to be willing to talk about your victories, your creativity, your strengths, and your skills in a way that enhances your reputation. It means that when you win something, you accept credit for it. When someone compliments you, you say "Thank you". When you want something, you ask for it, instead of waiting to be asked. It means that you don't have "group therapy" with your boss.

On social media this can be done simply with a photograph or an image. You can talk about how happy you were to win a difficult case, or thank everyone for their messages following an exciting promotion and talk about what you want to achieve. You can demonstrate your thinking as a leader. As writers always say – show, don't tell. Talk about yourself with confidence and conviction. It is an essential skill for building your reputation.

Note to the women reading this. Implicit biases about gender compliant behavior still abound in the business and legal world. This means that self-promotion that is viewed positively for men can be regarded as negative when done by a woman. This doesn't mean you don't self-promote if you are a woman. It simply means you should take this into account and decide how you want to handle it. Perhaps you calibrate your comments to your audience, perhaps you don't.

Finally, you have to determine what type of reputation you want – outside of being an excellent lawyer.

> *"I have tried to put myself out there. I want to be one of the lawyers whose name comes to mind when prospects or clients face a legal issue. This outreach has included writing papers and articles, speaking, commenting on legal issues reported in the press, making an effort to meet new people even in what seem to be purely social settings. But even more fundamentally, I have worked hard to get great results. Happy clients are my best 'sales representatives'."*
>
> Tim Long, shareholder, Greenberg Traurig

Are you the cerebral lawyer's lawyer? Are you the creative, out-of-the-box thinker? Are you a strategic genius who can figure a way out of any problem? Are you a bombastic trial lawyer or a quiet methodical trial lawyer? Are you the dealmaker for big corporate matters or the person who brings new businesses into the market? Or are you some combination of these?

Mollie Burks, a partner at Gordon & Rees, puts it this way:

> *"My brand is that I always put my clients' needs before everything and they know it. I care deeply about my clients and I make it clear that I am there to help them solve their problems."*

Once you determine the reputation you want to develop, you focus your reputation-building efforts in that direction – so that you are always working toward creating a reputation that matches your passion and that is true to who you are. This is known as creating your personal "brand"

and you should always be consistent in its presentation, whether in person or online. But, beware. If you aren't comfortable with the reputation you are trying to build, clients will recognize that and be put off. So, be yourself and promote the real you – not the person you think you should be.

Building your reputation in a remote working world

> *"The pandemic underscored and highlighted a truth that we have always known – it is important to stay in touch with people, reach out to people, see if they need support or help."*
>
> Joan Haratani, partner, Morgan Lewis

Allowing attorneys to work remotely has certainly been advantageous in many ways. But it can negatively impact the development of new lawyers and affect their ability to develop their skill sets as well as their reputations. By not being present in the office, attorneys miss opportunities to engage in discussions with more senior attorneys, to have informal interactions with partners, to be top of mind when new assignments come in, and to get to know colleagues professionally and personally. This lack of personal exposure to senior attorneys and partners can negatively impact the development of your reputation and your skills.

To counter that, and if you can, you should try to be in the office several days a week, particularly in your first few years. And you should use that time to engage with others, asking them about projects they are handling, volunteering to be of assistance to them, talking about your work, and participating in personal and professional conversations. If you can't be in the office, you should maximize your interactions on virtual calls – offering to do presentations, participating in client calls, asking for "zoom in person" feedback, rather than emails. You should also pick up the phone and call your colleagues, rather than simply emailing them as phone calls often lead to sharing more information than just the subject matter of the call.

You want senior attorneys and partners to get to know you, how you interact with others; you want them to know your skill set and your goals and aspirations; you want them to see you speak and think on your feet. All of these things can be done remotely, but are far more effective in person. So get out of your house and come to the office if you can!

Building your external reputation in a remote working environment requires focusing on what is important to your client during this time.

As mentioned previously, the pandemic has raised all kinds of new issues in the workplace. You can develop your reputation as an expert in one of those new areas by writing, providing webinars, blogging, and using social media to get out in front of the issues. As Debbie Epstein Henry, public speaker and consultant, DEH Consulting, Speaking and Writing, puts it:

> *"Online presence is critical for building your business – it's a means to be a resource to others, extend yourself generously, celebrate others, connect others, lend your voice, and showcase your work."*

This kind of communication is even more important in the remote work environment.

Here marketing is important. Think of checklists, executive summaries, and catchy headlines as ways to convey the new ideas you are promoting that will be easily accessible, because many in-house lawyers are overwhelmed with communications by email from outside lawyers. So differentiate yourself with clever ways of communicating the substance of your message. By devoting attention to the significant issues businesses are coping with due to the pandemic you can establish yourself as a relevant, creative, and innovative businessperson with legal expertise. And that is always the goal.

Chapter 4: Rainmaker traits – the secret sauce of business development

The second factor in becoming a successful rainmaker is the ability to build relationships, and, as noted above, that requires different skills from anything we are taught in law school. For some lawyers it comes naturally. But for most lawyers it requires some combination of learning the tactics involved in relationship building and enhancing the personal characteristics that make rainmakers successful. Those two things are inextricably intertwined.

The Rainmaking Study

In 2011, I decided to undertake a study to figure out how I – someone who is not particularly exceptional – could have built a sustainable multi-million-dollar book of business, while some of my colleagues – who were exceptional – had little to no business. My theory was that it took more than a great reputation and terrific legal skills to bring in clients.

I contacted a friend of mine, who I believe is one of the great thinkers on the future of the legal industry – William Henderson, professor of law at Indiana Maurer School of Law. At the time, Professor Henderson was focused on how law firms could improve the way they hire associates, in part, by identifying the personal characteristics that make lawyers successful at the firms by which they are being hired.

I asked him if he and his team would be willing to apply a similar analysis to rainmakers. He, along with his then business partner Caren Ulrich Stacy (another amazingly innovative and creative thinker about the legal industry), were up for the challenge. So, we began our study. The issue we were examining was whether rainmakers displayed distinct characteristics from other lawyers and, if so, could those characteristics be identified? We put together an advisory board composed of major law firms from across the country, and asked for their input on how to go about studying this issue. Professor Henderson and his team then set out to gather data.

We divided the world into rainmakers and client service partners. Rainmakers were lawyers who had generated over $4 million of business a year for a sustained period; client service partners were lawyers who were valuable to their firms but who didn't have their own books of business. We asked firms across the country to identify lawyers who fell into these two categories and that resulted in the identification of 300 partners. While we hoped to be able to gather data on men, women, and minority rainmakers, the criteria we established did not yield sufficient numbers of minority lawyers. Thus, the study's conclusions are limited to male and female rainmakers. We tested these partners, using psychometric tests measuring various personal characteristics. (These were tests commonly used to evaluate competency for sales positions. Of course, given the disdain most lawyers have for sales (see earlier), we did not tell the participants that they were taking sales-oriented tests.) We also did behavioral interviewing and gathered personal background information on 86 of these partners, 62 of whom were rainmakers and 24 of whom were client service partners. In these interviews, the research team explored the choices, attitudes, and behaviors of these partners relating to work and client development.

The study took two years to complete and was published by Lawyer Metrics in December 2014.[1] The results were compelling. We confirmed that rainmakers display different characteristics from client service partners. We also found male and female rainmakers possess the same characteristics – there was no difference in the results based on gender. As an interesting aside, we found that most firms offer special business development training to women attorneys based on the assumption that the lack of women rainmakers is the result of a lack of training. Yet the Rainmaking Study suggests that women do not need special training. My theory is that it is the system of dispersing client opportunities, of assigning lead roles in cases, of passing on institutional clients, etc. that contributes to the lack of women rainmakers, not a lack of skill on the part of the women. The background and behavioral interviewing provided surprising insights into what kinds of life experiences influence the development of the characteristics that make rainmakers successful.

For example, we found that rainmakers didn't necessarily go to elite law schools; were not necessarily on law review, but got good grades; often came from blue collar families; worked during their school years either because they had to or because they wanted to; and most were married or had long-term partners. We did find one difference in the marital status of rainmakers: the male rainmakers, for the most part, had non-working spouses or partners, while the female rainmakers had spouses or partners who worked outside the house.

The key traits of the successful rainmaker

According to the Rainmaking Study, the personal characteristics that rainmakers have in common, and that differentiate them from client service partners, are described by the following terms:

- Engagement;
- Dominance;
- Motivation; and
- Risk-taking.

It is the combination of these personal characteristics and certain background factors that makes rainmakers different from client service partners and makes them successful at bringing in business. But the ways in which rainmakers use these personal characteristics differ from person to person. While this seems obvious, it is important to say out loud because lawyers are often looking for a check-the-box sheet. That doesn't apply to rainmaking; there is no "one size fits all". Every person must develop his or her own style that is authentic to that person. You can't imitate me, nor I you, because clients will know when you aren't being sincere or true to yourself. I am an extrovert, and I am comfortable walking into a room where I don't know anyone. I can start a conversation and keep it going with most people. Because of that, the way I display the characteristics identified in the Rainmaking Study may be 180 degrees different from the way another equally or more successful rainmaker displays these characteristics.

So, these characteristics – which are discussed in detail in the next chapters – give you a framework and insight into the types of personal behaviors that will make you successful as a rainmaker. Some people will come by these traits naturally, while for others these characteristics will have to be developed and practiced. That takes time and commitment, but most people will be able to find ways to embrace these characteristics and use them to enhance their business development efforts.

On the other hand, it is important to note that not everyone can or should be a rainmaker. Client service partners – the people who provide the support for the work the rainmakers bring in – are critical components of any firm structure. Rainmakers rely on client service partners and cannot survive without them. Unless I have a strong, reliable, and dependable team in the office, I can't bring in significant clients. So, people who don't have the skills to be rainmakers, or simply don't want to be rainmakers, often become the client service partners without whom the rainmakers cannot survive! And if I were in charge of things, these client service partners would be recognized and rewarded more consistently with the value they bring to our teams.

The overriding message is this: rainmakers are successful because they are comfortable developing business. They love bringing in clients; they are interested in people, in business, and in winning. As one of the best in the business describes how it feels to be a rainmaker:

> *"Rainmaking is like a box of chocolates. The anticipation of the first bite (or 'ask') is both exhilarating and precarious. But once you get a caramel (or a 'yes') you realize that the risk was definitely worth it."*
>
> Caren Ulrich Stacy, CEO, Diversity Lab

References

1 The Rainmaking Study can be accessed here: https://s3.amazonaws.com/tld-documents.llnassets.com/0006000/6482/rainmaker_study.pdf. It gives a detailed account of the types of tests we administered and the statistical information we gathered.

Chapter 5: Engagement – the art of active listening

Have you ever been in a conversation where you felt the other person – who was standing in front of you – just wasn't listening? How could you tell? Perhaps by the blank stare, the lack of response, and/or the eyes that divert to something across the room? That person is not engaged, and you know it when you see it.

Engagement is one of the most critical behaviors for effective business development. It is best defined as being "interested and interesting", and it involves a skill that is waning in our society where looking at our phones occupies more of our time than looking at the people with whom we are interacting. That skill is active listening. It means when someone is talking, you are looking at them and actually listening – listening for information, tone, subtext, and inflection – while also taking in body language.

To let the person with whom you are interacting know that you are listening, you need to show your involvement: nod, ask questions, respond appropriately to the information being shared. So, when a person says, "I just came back from vacation" your response should be, "Where did you go?" followed by, "Did your kids go with you?" or "What was your favorite part of the trip?" or "Where did you stay?" or all those questions and more. Showing interest in what the person is saying requires asking questions and sharing thoughts.

> *"I enjoy finding out who people are and understanding different kinds of people. People are far more engaging than the law."*
>
> Robert Stein, formerly of counsel, Coblentz Patch Duffy & Bass LLP

This may seem elementary. But there are a surprising number of lawyers who don't understand the importance of this kind of small talk or who are so self-centered that they respond to "I like Italian food" with a long story that starts out with, "I do, too, and I cook it all the time. Just the other day I had a dinner party…" – droning on and on about themselves and their cooking skills without seeking any information from the other person. It is exactly the same on social media. If you just post about yourself without acknowledging and responding to the successes and achievements of others, then the impression it leaves is the same. It all registers to a potential client as someone who is not interested and not interesting. And that may be a non-starter for many clients who want to hire attorneys not only who are excellent at their craft, but also with whom they want to spend time.

Active listening for a formal pitch

This active listening skill becomes even more important when actually pitching a client for business. In a formal pitch setting, attorneys send over all their well-designed documents about their firms, their practices, and their victories. They bring a slew of colleagues who share information about the global breadth of the firm, the many different practice areas, the wonderful culture of the firm, and the role they hope to play partnering with this client and becoming a trusted advisor. And they talk at the client, answering questions as they occur, but basically telling the client why their firm is the best for this engagement.

The active listener approaches this event differently.

Pre-pitch

First, she contacts the potential client in advance of the pitch and asks the following questions:

1. How long do we have?
2. Who will be there?
3. What other firms are being considered?
4. What are the most critical issues to address during the pitch?
5. What kinds of materials can we bring about our firm that would be useful to you?

While asking these questions, the rainmaker is also asking follow-up questions, commenting on the responses from the client, and beginning to show her personality.

Not all clients will allow this initial contact. And even if they do, they may not respond to all of these questions. But it is rare that a client will fault an attorney who tries to ensure that the presentation they are being asked to make is relevant and focused on what the client wants to hear.

Even if it is "normal" to include a brochure with standard information about the firm, this may not be appropriate for all clients. I was moderating a panel discussion on rainmaking and I asked one of the general counsel on the panel whether she likes to get glossy brochures or PowerPoints about the firm. Her response was this: "You know what I do with those? I throw them in the trash". Another general counsel on a different panel said she rarely reads them but she does keep them on her desk. When asked what she does after they begin to pile up she said, without pausing, "Oh, I throw them out". This is why the question, "What kinds of materials would be useful?" is one you want to get an answer to in your pre-pitch phone call.

Focusing the pitch presentation

Second, the active listener prepares for the pitch by focusing on the information she thinks the client will want to hear, based on the reason for the pitch.

As an active listener, you will want to be sure to focus your pitch presentation – from the pitch team to the opening comments to the materials you bring – on the issues that are relevant to the reason you are there. You may think it is critical to let the client know what a large footprint your firm has, the many states or countries in which your firm has offices, your various awards, etc., but the client most likely knows all of that. That is why you were invited to pitch for the business in the first place.

So, when you prepare for the pitch, spend your time thinking about what will distinguish you from your competitors, what will make you stand out, what you can do to show that you can be a trusted advisor to this client, that you understand their business, that you are a problem solver who can help the client realize their business goals in a legal, cost-effective way. For example, if the matter involves a complaint that has been filed and the client has said he or she wants to talk about how your firm will approach the issue, consider bringing to the pitch a draft answer or demurrer or motion to dismiss – or a proposed litigation plan, with a timeline and alternatives to litigation. And when you hand this over, engage with the client. Ask what he thinks of this approach. In fact, it is important to remember that many in-house lawyers are skilled practitioners, who expect to be treated as such. So, show them that you value their opinion and judgment – that if he or she hires your firm, you will treat them as an equal partner.

Spending time online researching all those present at the pitch can substantially help you in the way you present to them. There is a wealth of information available about individuals, from their hobbies to their careers. Showing interest throughout the pitch by recognizing them as people will differentiate you. For example, you might share a similar hobby or have attended the same high school. These are all points of connection. Just make sure you don't look like a stalker! There is a great story about an attorney who, in researching a potential client, learned that he had gone to Penn. The attorney making the pitch walked into the room and the first thing he said was, "How did you like living in Philadelphia?". The potential client was taken aback, as he lived in New York and was in his seventies. After a few awkward moments, the attorney disclosed that he knew the client went to Penn, which is why he was asking the question. The potential client thought this was quite odd and was offended that the attorney was "looking him up". Of course, the reference to Penn could have been used at some later point in the conversation, but right out of the box it was a little creepy and off-putting!

Also, do not assume that the highest-titled person in the room is necessarily the decision-maker. Many general counsel defer decisions about outside counsel to the person in charge of the case or matter. So, unless you know who will make the decision about the firm to be hired, direct your comments to everyone in the room as though any one of them could be determining your future

Setting the tone

The successful rainmaker will set the tone for the meeting as a discussion, not a lecture. The mistake a lot of lawyers make in formal pitch settings is that they talk too much and don't listen. That is not engagement; that is pontification.

> *"Too many people approach every interaction thinking about themselves, winning, and being convincing – they tend to talk more, ask fewer questions and generally fail at building trust and rapport. In contrast, people who are the most successful, approach every interaction with curiosity, confidence and humility. Their mantra is: How can I be of service?"*
>
> Catherine McCluskey Zinn, chief client officer, Baker Botts

Listening is a large part of making a pitch successful. So, set the tone at the beginning of the meeting. Confirm the time frame, acknowledging that the in-house person has a busy schedule that you want to respect, and then stick to their time frame, calibrating your presentation if you need to so that you make sure you don't run over your time. The best thing you can hear at the end of your allotted time is "Let's keep talking".

After confirming the time frame, you again defer to the client by acknowledging the reason you are at the pitch but asking for her guidance in identifying the most important issues to her:

> *"We are prepared to talk about the recent case filed against you, but we want to make sure we answer whatever issues are most pressing to you. So, if you think it would be useful, maybe we can start by addressing what most concerns you about this matter."*

> Or, *"In our previous conversations before coming today, you mentioned you were most interested in discussion X. Is that still true or would you rather we start with something else?"*

The client may not want to answer this question, but if she does, your job is to listen closely and tailor your response and presentation to address those issues first – don't retreat to your prepared script.

The rest of the pitch should be a lot of back and forth with you and the client – you asking questions and responding to the client, the client asking questions and you responding. A one-way narrative by you is far less effective than an exchange where both you and the client are actively engaged.

Also, avoid the common phrases people use in pitches that have no meaning. But if you want to use them, explain what you mean.

Wrong: "We partner with our clients."

Right: "We partner with our clients by making sure we fully understand their business. To that end, if you retain our firm, we would want to come out – on our dime – and see the facility and how your business operates. That gives us the opportunity to give practical and tailored advice and counsel that makes sense for your business."

Wrong: "We will be your trusted advisor."

Right: "We want to assure you that we understand our role, which is to give you the best legal advice we can to help you realize your business goals. Let me give you an example of where we were able to help another client reach his desired objective…"

Wrong: "We are committed to diversity."

Right: Do not underestimate the importance of diversity in the selection process used by outside counsel. When Michelle Banks, former general counsel at Gap Inc. was asked what she looks for in outside counsel she said, among other things, "*Share values in three key areas: Diversity, Pro Bono, and Integrity*". True commitment to these "soft" issues can make or break your chances of getting the business from some clients.

While you may want to include some statements about diversity in your pitch or discussion with a potential client (especially since this is becoming, for many clients, a significant factor in distinguishing firms), the strongest message you can send is to bring a team that is diverse and to make it clear that the diverse attorneys are not just there for show. Clients are now familiar with the game some firms play of bringing women and minorities to the pitch and never seeing them again. Some clients may even ask whether the diverse members of the team will have speaking roles on the matter being discussed or whether they will get origination credit. You should come ready to discuss those kinds of issues as well as your firm's commitment to diversity.

Diversity on legal teams is fast becoming an important factor to many in-house counsel when deciding between firms. In fact, in-house counsel have realized how much power they have in shaping the teams that do work for their companies and they are flexing that muscle when choosing their outside lawyers. As a result, some demand diversity on the teams, whilst others may simply reject firms that show up to pitch for cases with all white males. You ignore this at your peril.

It is important to make sure these messages are consistent right the way across your personal and firm profiles – on your website, the images on social media, the webinar events you run. Clients will look and they will make a judgment if they are not consistent, i.e. you are not honest about your commitment to an issue.

Post-pitch

After the pitch, the rainmaker follows up with the client.

Remember when your parents made you write "thank you" notes after you received a gift, to underscore your gratitude for the present? That same principle applies here. After a formal pitch, you should send a follow-up note – preferably hand-written. In these days of electronic communications that overwhelm many of us, a hand-written note stands out and differentiates you from other lawyers. It seems and feels personal because it takes a type of thought and effort that emails or texts do not.

If you have been listening actively, there is probably something that you can mention in this note that will answer a question that was unanswered in the meeting, or reference something that came up during the meeting. It could be something substantive like a website that has information relevant to an issue you discussed, or something more mundane like a review of a restaurant that came up at the pitch. But even just a written note saying, essentially, "Thank you for considering our firm" will remind the client of you and, hopefully, distinguish you from firms that do not send that thank you.

It is always best, of course, to leave the meeting with an "assignment" to follow up on something that came up in the meeting – a case citation, an article, or an introduction to another in-house counsel who had a similar issue and used you. In any case, it is good to have some piece of information to get back to the client with that will give you the opportunity to connect again.

> *"I take notes as a reminder of how I plan to follow-up and then I do so. Additionally, I try to keep the potential client top of mind and keep in regular touch, e.g. inviting him/her to events, sharing relevant articles, making introductions and providing opportunities for visibility, speaking, writing, etc."*
>
> Deborah Epstein Henry, public speaker and consultant, DEH Consulting, Speaking, Writing

Active listening in casual interactions

Active listening skills are not just for formal pitches. This skill should be applied in all aspects of client development and client relationships – zoom meetings, lunches, dinners, conferences, networking events. You should always be taking in what the person is saying so that you learn what is important to them, what they are worried about, and how they think.

For existing clients, showing an interest in the person and what matters to her is critical. For example, if the client is nervous about an upcoming promotion, you might want to volunteer to make a call to her boss to offer praise for her work. In fact, you might want to do that even if the client isn't up for a promotion! If the client indicates that her boss dislikes outside counsel bills exceeding budgeted amounts, you want to make sure to monitor that client's bills closely and provide a heads-up when it looks like there may be a problem sticking to the budget. Remember, your job is to make the client look good, so you should be thinking about her career and the people to whom she must answer as you develop the relationship and do work for her.

It is also important, however, to listen for personal issues that are important to the client. So, remembering a client's birthday with a card or note may be something you want to do. Similarly, if the client is dealing with a sick parent, you might want to ask how things are going the next time you see or speak with the client. If a client has a child who loves baseball, you might want to offer baseball tickets to an upcoming game. Lawyers often offer to take clients to sporting events. But many clients find this annoying rather than enticing. Why? Because they have lives and families and going to a baseball game with one's attorney takes away from the client's personal time and from his/her family. So, offering the tickets for a "family outing" may inure more to your benefit in that you are acknowledging that the client has a personal life!

The challenges posed by remote working are many, but also can be useful in connecting with clients and in showing your active listening skills. So, don't be reluctant, for example, to invite a client to a "zoom" social function – send a glass with a bottle of mixer for the event, or include "bar snacks" and a recipe for a drink, or send a nice bag of coffee, a gift card for food delivery, a bottle of wine, to your client with a date and time to share in this zoom outing. The possibilities are endless. But use this to show you are engaged and listening to your client and what he/she needs. For example, I had a lawyer who used me frequently as a mediator. He joked about how he missed the snacks provided by my company during mediations because the mediations were no longer in person. So the next time I mediated with him, I sent him – and opposing counsel – a box of snacks and a gift card for lunch to be delivered during the mediation. Not only did the attorneys find it funny, but it showed the attorney who had "complained" that I was listening to him. Those kinds of gestures go a long way.

The point is this: Clients don't exist in a vacuum. They exist in the same world as we do, and they are facing the same professional and personal challenges we have all faced. Being thoughtful and considerate and following up on issues that are important to the client at work and at home shows that you pay attention and that you care about the client as a person as well as a source of business.

Making the connection

Rainmakers are also natural connectors. That is, they can't help themselves from hearing one thing and connecting it to another. This ability to recognize and identify connections is an extension of active listening that shows the client that there are benefits to the relationship. Sometimes, making these kinds of connections enhances your professional reputation with the client. For example, if a potential client says, "I am going to see one of my attorneys in San Francisco", the rainmaker – who is actively listening – says, "Wow, while you are in San Francisco, you might want to meet my friend there who has just come out of a merger like the one you went through". You are not only making a potentially important connection for the client, from which they may benefit, but you are also showing that you have some expertise in the subject area.

Other times making a connection enhances your personal relationship with the client. So, when a potential client says, "I am thinking of moving to Dallas because my fiancé just got transferred", the rainmaker says, "I have two really good friends there who can give you the low down on where to live as well as the great restaurants, etc". These kinds of connections are important because they will likely distinguish you from the many lawyers who think mostly about making connections that benefit them, not the client. It is not necessarily a bad thing to ask clients to make connections for you. For example, a good way to build a reputation in an industry is to ask a current client to introduce you to a potential client in another company. But, it is refreshing for in-house counsel to have an outside lawyer thinking about how she can help the in-house counsel succeed in her own life.

That is why looking for connections is a hallmark trait of a rainmaker. Thinking of opportunities for clients to meet colleagues from other companies, helping a client who wants to look for a new position by introducing her to a headhunter, making an introduction to a Facebook group online, recommending a pre-school or college counsellor or elder care helper are the kinds of connections that go a long way toward building relationships.

> *"I first try to understand the business of the potential client as well as the potential client's needs and frustrations. I then see how I can be a resource, both for the potential client's business needs as well as in response to other interests or needs the potential client may have. I also try to see how I can connect the potential client to others who may be able to help."*
>
> Deborah Epstein Henry, public speaker and consultant,
> DEH Consulting, Speaking, Writing

Doing things that you like to do as "client development"

The overused words "be authentic" are actually relevant to the engagement characteristic that all rainmakers possess. Why? You can't really be engaged if you are doing things that make you uncomfortable or in which you are not interested. Those types of things make client development seem like a chore.

The key to engagement is making client development part of your life. But that requires that you broaden your concept of client development. For example, a client development tool that shows true engagement can be a phone call that goes like this: "Hi, Sue. I know your first child just went off to college. I remember how that felt. Makes you realize how fast time flies. How are you doing?" There is no mention of business, there is no "ask". There is simply a showing of empathy and interest in the person. It can't be faked, however. It must be real.

Similarly, the ability to show engagement can come from everyday activities. For example, I love to cook and entertain. It is not stressful or difficult for me to put on a dinner party or a large party. So, when my kids were little I would entertain clients at my house, invite them to my holiday parties, include them in birthday parties and graduation celebrations – events that were part of my family life. And I would invite them and their families, which cemented relationships that lasted throughout my career.

> *"I like to include spouses and kids in social events. I think clients really appreciate that since they are away from their families enough."*
>
> Heidi Friedman, partner, Thompson Hine LLP

I also found ways to integrate my desire to be involved in school events with client development activities. I ran the local school carnival for six years by delegating responsibilities for the nuts and bolts to other parents in the community. I served on the board of trustees for my kids' schools so that I could be involved in decisions that affected their education. And in doing these things, I got the personal satisfaction of being part of my children's school life as well as the opportunity to meet people in my community who had the ability to give out business for their companies or to make introductions to those people. Note, however: I didn't do these things to get business, but some business flowed from the personal relationships I developed with people in these non-business and casual settings.

> *"What kinds of social events help deepen client relationships? Any social event where you can have one-on-one time and not discuss business. Legal issues will come up for discussion while you are building a personal relationship."*
>
> Tim Long, shareholder, Greenberg Taurig LLP

> *"I approach business development by planning events that I would like to attend. I like to host events that are social… the business comes from the connections that flow from the events."*
>
> Anne Cappella, partner, Weil, Gotshal & Manges LLP

Engagement is one of the most important aspects of client development. It comes naturally to some lawyers, but for others it is a stretch to listen and not talk, to be interested in the person from whom you want to get business, to think about the client and what you can do for him/her instead of what the client can do for you, and to find connections and opportunities for others.

In addition to my law practice, I have also become a prominent voice on issues relating to women lawyers. I am passionate about keeping women in the legal profession. As a result, it often comes up in conversations with clients – either because they know about my work or because they say something that sparks me to talk about my work. And that can be a powerful connection that can influence a decision to retain you.

> *"[A potential client] heard me speak, knew from that speech both that I was involved in New Jersey Women Lawyers Association and was a smart employment lawyer, which her growing company, of which she was the general counsel, needed at the time. She wanted to get more involved in women's issues as well, so she called a smart lawyer who shared her interests. I have been representing her companies ever since and we have become good friends."*
>
> Galit Kierkut, shareholder, Greenberg Traurig

To hone your engagement skills, spend time in everyday conversations, not talking about yourself unless asked, and truly listening to what the other person is saying. This is a skill that can be learned, but it takes practice. I sometimes play a game at parties where I don't know a lot of people. I make it a point not to say a thing about myself unless asked. I am not rude; I just don't volunteer information. What is remarkable about this game is that I can go through an entire party with people never asking me where I am from, what I do, if I have kids, etc. What does that say? It says I am a good rainmaker because I have gathered a lot of information about other people. It also says that the people at the party are not very good rainmakers because they expressed no interest in getting to know me. Try it sometime – it's fascinating! The good news is that your daily interactions with people give you plenty of opportunities to develop this skill so that it becomes second nature.

Exhibiting these characteristics in a remote working world

As mentioned above, there are some advantages that have come with remote working and one of those advantages is in the area of engagement. While that may seem like an odd thing to say, it is true. We now have a common experience to talk about that is appropriate for both genders, for all ethnicities and races, and at all levels of the firm or an organization. Why? Because we have a shared experience where we all faced the same problems and challenges – how we coped with the isolation, whether we got COVID, how we managed childcare, how safe (or not) we are feeling as the pandemic perhaps comes to an end. This gives us common ground to start conversations and to get insight and give insight to each other on how we manage adversity and stress.

Use this communal experience to engage with colleagues and clients. It gives you an excuse for calling someone to ask how they are doing, for example. And then, you can move the conversation to business issues:

> *"Hey Joe, it's Pat. I was just thinking of you as I was off to pick up my kid (again) from preschool, as she has been exposed to COVID. I know you have a couple of kids – how are you doing in that regard? We have really had to scramble a couple of times with these unexpected shutdowns. I imagine it is also wreaking havoc in the workplace too. How are you all handling these kinds of issues for your workers…"*

The remote work model that has resulted from the pandemic also provides opportunities for new areas of expertise – privacy rights, security issues, whistleblower claims, leave issues, OSHA regulations, real estate deals, etc. There are many possibilities to develop an expertise in the challenges posed by the pandemic. Don't miss those chances! Think out of the box.

"Business development is as important as ever for women's careers. With so many of us spending a good chunk of our week working remotely, it's critical to take advantage of Zoom, Teams, and other online platforms to cultivate the personal relationships that really matter when it comes to growing business."

Stephanie S. Scharf, partner, Scharf Banks Marmor LLC and principal, The Red Bee Group, LLC

Chapter 6: Dominance – focusing on the solution, not the problem

Dominance is a critical component of a rainmaker's style because it is how you prove your worth to the client or potential client. It is how you show you are truly a business partner with the client, adding the legal expertise in addition to the business savvy that will help the client advance her business goals.

But, although this characteristic is called "dominance", it is really about persuasion – the ability to effectively help the client to make business decisions that are legal and that will achieve their business goals. Some lawyers think they can achieve this by "wowing" clients with their legal prowess, so they use legal jargon and Latin phrases to impress and, in their minds, persuade the client that she should defer to the lawyer's expertise. But, in truth, that pretense doesn't resonate with most businesspeople. They are looking for legal solutions to their business problems. They want their lawyers to talk about how they can achieve their business goals. And that is no different whether it is for content online or meetings in person. Demonstrating your understanding of business first and foremost and the problems they face is key.

That is why successful rainmakers are those lawyers who realize that our legal education is a tool to use and share with clients to further their business objectives. Just as an accountant might advise a company on the best tax strategy for the company to pursue to meet its business goal of lessening tax payments, our job is to advise the company on the best legal strategy to adopt to accomplish certain business objectives.

Giving that kind of advice is grounded in not only knowing but also understanding the business goals of our clients or potential clients. To do that, we have to understand their business. What does that mean? It means we must be able to contextualize the problem in the business we are advising. By understanding the business, rainmakers can use creative and strategic thinking to lead the client to the business solution that meets their goals and is legally viable.

Know the business of your client

When I was in-house at Bank of America, our general counsel made every single lawyer work in a branch office of the bank for two weeks. Sounds silly, right? But it's not. Our general counsel knew that if we were going to be effective business advisors, we had to understand what our business partners did. And so we learned the business of banking, up close and personal. Since this was back in the day, before ATMs and internet banking, when people came into the branches to cash checks, withdraw money, get loans, etc. we lawyers were working in the heart of the banking business. And we learned what that business was all about by doing the jobs of the people in the branches. It was a fast-track learning curve, but it was invaluable to ensuring that we quickly developed a sense of what bankers do, the obstacles and challenges they face in performing their jobs, and the specialized knowledge necessary to do their jobs. With that knowledge we were in a much better position to advise our client groups as questions arose.

After I left my in-house position, I incorporated this idea into my own client development efforts. For many potential clients I would offer, "on my dime", to come to their facilities to see how they operated, to spend time with their managers to see the kinds of issues they dealt with on a day-to-day basis, to gain an understanding of how they produced their "product", whether that was a bottle of wine or a loan to a customer.

By doing this I not only differentiated myself from other lawyers, but I also was more effective at counseling my clients on business issues they were facing. Now, granted, I am an employment lawyer – so seeing first-hand how the business operates was directly relevant to many of the issues on which I had to advise. But this process of learning the client's business allowed me to speak in the language of the client, to visualize the setting in which the problem was arising, and to better understand the reason for the business goal the client was trying to achieve. That kind of information is important and provides insight into your client's business, regardless of your practice area. And that makes you better able to help your client choose the best path to viable and legal business solutions.

Think like a lawyer, but don't talk like one

Always keep in mind that clients and potential clients are talking to us not because they have nothing better to do, but because they have or anticipate having a legal problem that may interfere with their business goals.

Your job is to find a way to say, "Yes, you can execute the business strategy" (unless it is illegal) and then to assess the legal risks associated with the proposed strategy. The mistake most lawyers make when pitching for a new case or advising a new or existing client, however, is that they spend time "issue spotting" and thinking out loud about the parade of horrible legal scenarios that could result from the proposed strategy.

That can be frustrating for the client and isn't useful. Your job is to be the problem-solver, not the naysayer. So, the successful rainmaker approaches challenging issues as follows:

- Listens to the client's proposed plan;
- Prods the client for more information to ascertain the reasons for the plan, the depth of the commitment to the plan, and the business consequences that could arise if the plan is not implemented; and
- Then thinks about possible ways to accomplish the plan that don't involve saying "No".

The rainmaker understands that her job is not to pontificate on the applicable law or legal standards but to talk in plain English and in business terms about the ways in which the business goals can be accomplished. The rainmaker is innovative and creative in the way she approaches business problems – solutions-oriented, strategic, showing initiative, and finding a way to say "Yes".

I usually use the Goldilocks approach to advising clients – I offer them three options: the most risky, the least risky, and the one in the middle. But I make it clear that I am willing to do any of these options so that they know I am there to serve them and do what is best for their business, not what might ensure a legal win for me.

For example, if a potential client exhibits an appetite for bringing a counterclaim against someone who has sued them, I would not say, "Not a good idea" (even though I may think it is a terrible idea). Instead, I would assure them that I am happy to pursue that approach (unless it is illegal or unethical). But I would then try to understand their motivation, and their real goal, and whether there is a less expensive, less time-consuming, less divisive, and less aggressive way to accomplish that goal. I then suggest the three possible approaches. For example, in this scenario, I might propose the following: the countersuit approach, a less in-your-face approach that still meets the client's objectives, and trying to resolve the dispute informally, before either side gets too entrenched and before money is spent chasing what may be an unachievable goal.

Nine times out of ten, the client will reconsider the initial high-risk strategy and go for one of the less confrontational approaches – because for most businesses, that is what makes the most sense. For that to happen, however, the client has to believe (because it is true) that you are committed to pursuing whichever approach the client wants. The client also must know that you appreciate the business objective he or she is trying to achieve. That is called trust, and is grounded in the client's confidence that you are looking out for what is best for the company because you know and understand the business, the players, the business objectives for this matter, and the politics of the organization.

I also do this in a pitch situation. Either I find out before the pitch what the client wants and why, and then have my team come prepared with creative solutions to reach that goal, or if I haven't had the opportunity to find out in advance what the client is trying to achieve, I have the discussion on the spot – brainstorming with my team and the client on the alternatives and options that should be considered. This shows the client how we work and think, and gets them invested in the solutions.

Chapter 7: Motivation – empowering your team and your client

Bringing your client into the team

Rainmakers are team players, but in a way that is different from client service partners. Rainmakers view the team of attorneys in their firms to be important and necessary to the product they are selling. And the team must be able to provide excellent and responsive legal advice to the clients who are brought into the firm by the rainmaker. However, making sure that the legal work is done correctly and efficiently is not the best and highest use of the rainmaker's time. And frankly, the testing done in conjunction with the Rainmaking Study shows that ensuring the "trains run on time" is not at the top of the rainmaker's skill set. On the other hand, client service partners generally possess these kinds of skills and are quite good at them. So, good rainmakers empower and delegate client service partners to run the team in the office.

That means rainmakers bring the clients into the firm and are the primary interface with the client once the matter begins; client service partners are responsible for ensuring that the team in the office is running smoothly, efficiently, and in a cost-effective manner. Thus, while strategic decisions are made by the client, the rainmaker and the team, the client service partner makes sure that the strategy is implemented, that the team is responsive to all inquiries from the client, that the client has sufficient time to review documents before they are finalized, that clients are kept informed of changes in scheduling or deadlines, and that any glitches or potential problems are identified early to the rainmaker and the client for discussion and resolution. In short, client service partners are the "chief operating officers" for the rainmakers – they are essential to the success of the team.

While I, as the rainmaker, recognize the importance of my team in the office, I have another teammate – the client. I want to make sure that the client feels she is part of the team. So I interface frequently with her on the big picture issues: how she is feeling about the overall strategy, where there is a potential for resolution, monitoring, and considering the public and employee relations implications of the matter at hand as well as the impact on the business. I invite clients to participate in team meetings so that they can hear and opine in discussions about the course of the litigation. Clearly, not all clients want this level of involvement. But many in-house counsel are accomplished litigators and they welcome the opportunity to be part of the "team", so I treat them like another partner on the case. Most clients also want someone who, in the words of Heidi Friedman, partner at Thompson Hine LLP, "*understands budgeting, legal project management and the fact that the legal department is a cost center and costs must be controlled*". So, the rainmaker puts processes in place to ensure she is fully aware of how much things are costing, and warns the client in advance of potential significant or unexpected costs. To in-house lawyers, budget busting is a huge problem. Any way you can assist them with staying within their financial expectation makes you a valuable and savvy partner.

I take this one step further. Just as I use my law partners to bounce ideas off, I also use my clients to help me evaluate a strategy or an approach on cases that don't involve them or their company. So I might call a client up and say, "I am thinking of using this theme in my opening statement, what do you think?" or "I am having trouble coming up with a creative solution to this problem, and I wanted to pick your brain".

I do this because I value the opinions of my clients, but it has a secondary effect that is beneficial to building the all-important relationship with my clients – it confirms that I view them as part of my larger team. They understand that I am seeking them out because I respect their opinions and their expertise.

This cannot be effective if you aren't serious about wanting the client's input. But if you do value their opinions and insights, it is a great way to let your client know that your relationship is deeper than just attorney and client. It is a true partnership and team of equals.

Involving the client

Here is how this works in real life. A few years ago, I was helping Client A with a very difficult legal issue around a potential claim of religious discrimination. I called Client B, whose opinion I truly valued because he is one of the smartest people I know. We discussed the issues and he came up with some terrific ideas about how we might get around the legal problem Client A was facing. Several days later, I got a call from Client B saying that he had "done a little research" and had some additional ideas. Again, his insights were invaluable – it was like having another partner on the team! I thanked him and he then thanked me for making him feel so valued. That is the kind of thing that cements a relationship forever.

This involvement of the client in a broader relationship can also be done via social media (although obviously not on confidential matters). It may not be as personal, but it still conveys the message that you are open to others' ideas and support. People are always keen to give help and advice. This can open the door to new relationships, if you are responsive to people's replies.

Chapter 8: Risk-taking – the joy of taking chances

Risk-taking and engagement are probably the two most important characteristics for a rainmaker. We have already talked about engagement, so let's talk about risk.

Here is a truism – you cannot develop business unless you are willing to put yourself, your firm, and your reputation on the line. But this can be intimidating. In fact:

> *"The fear of rejection inhibits many lawyers in their business development efforts. No one likes to hear 'No'."*
>
> Roberta D. Liebenberg, partner, Fine, Kaplan and Black, RPC

Clearly, the risk most people associate with business development is that someone will not choose them, whether that be the potential client for a new case, the existing client who has a new matter, or the senior partner who is going on a pitch or appointing someone to be lead counsel.

So, this is where the rubber meets the road when it comes to who will be the successful rainmaker. The true rainmaker does not worry about not being chosen, because when rainmakers are told "No", they hear "Not now". And so, the rainmaker can take the hit, move on, and come back again at the appropriate time. That requires resilience, it requires grit, and that is what it takes to be a rainmaker.

Become fearless

One way to overcome a fear is to ask, "What is the worst thing that can happen?" Because as Joan Haratani, partner at Morgan Lewis, puts it, "*If you don't ask the question, the answer is always no*". In the context of business development, here is a partial list of "worst things":

- Your bid for the business is rejected.
- You are embarrassed when your colleagues find out you failed.

- You feel bad.
- You have wasted your time and energy.
- You are discouraged and have self-doubt going forward.

But what if you looked at it from a different perspective? From the "glass half full" perspective? Then these negatives become positives:

- You had a chance to share your experience and expertise with someone who can provide you with business in the future.
- Your colleagues know you are interested in bringing in new business.
- You have developed a pitch style or materials or an elevator speech that you can further refine and use in other potential engagements.
- You have more information about what works and what doesn't in trying to develop business.

"I don't see failure as a negative, honestly... there is really no reason to fear 'failure' because the nuggets of wisdom that you learn from your so-called failure are invaluable. Now if you make the same mistakes repeatedly, that's all on you."

Joan Haratani, partner, Morgan, Lewis & Bockius LLP

The trick to risk-taking in business development is using every opportunity to hone your skills and your message. And the more you do that, the better you are at pitching business. Of course, no one likes to be rejected. But that is just part of the game. You have to be willing to lose so you can learn how to win.

The hard part

As mentioned above, every time you ask for business you are putting yourself, your firm, your reputation, your record, and your ego on the line. That is the name of the game. To be effective, you must feel comfortable talking about yourself and your firm and why you should be chosen. For some, this kind of talk comes naturally. But others struggle with how to promote themselves, how to ask for business, and how to seal the deal.

There is something else, however, that makes risk-taking hard – and that is the existence of intentional and implicit bias. We know this exists – the client who wants someone who "looks like a lawyer" (e.g. white, male, gray hair, fit) and rejects anyone who doesn't fit that mold. This can be done intentionally or, even more often, through the application of biases that we all have, but don't necessarily know we are utilizing in our decision-making.

How do you overcome that? By knowing those prejudices are out there and by demonstrating through your communications and actions that you are every bit as qualified as the more "traditional" looking lawyer. You want to present as yourself, but know your audience. How you dress, how you talk, how you engage with the potential client can convey as much as your credentials and the materials you bring with you to a pitch or client meeting. You want to show the client that you understand him or her, that you are relatable, that you are capable, and that you have the qualifications and experience to do the job.

For example, if I am meeting with a tech company to pitch my firm, I am going to dress differently and speak differently from how I would behave if I were meeting with a large financial institution. My message would be the same, but how I deliver it depends on my audience. So when presenting to a hip, boutique hotel chain, I am going to be clever in the way I present any materials – not using the standard marketing stuff, but using different approaches that show innovative thinking and creativity. That presentation for a large financial institution would show creativity and innovation as well, but in a much more traditional way.

The biases that women and people of color face in client development are real, and despite our belief that people are becoming more sensitive to these issues, we have a long way to go. You have to do your best to recognize the possibility of these biases coming into play and go out of your way to disrupt those biases in a way that is authentic to you, but resonates with your audience.

Talking about yourself

If I had to identify one area where there is a difference between men's and women's business development skills, it would be their willingness to sell themselves. Women can sell the firm, the practice area, and the track record of the practice group. But when it comes to selling themselves many are scared to death. Why?

One of the primary reasons for this is the "P" standard to which women hold themselves. That is, the need to be perfect. And the fear of being seen as anything less than perfect often holds women back.

> *"Women may be wise to be more concerned with potential failure; there is some evidence that women's failures are remembered longer than men's. But that kind of bias may lead us to become too afraid of failure – avoiding it more than is needed, and in ways that don't serve our career goals."*
>
> Tara Sophia Mohr[1]

So, here is the internal dialogue for a woman versus a man in considering the "risk" associated with pitching for a new case:

The woman: I have second chaired a number of these cases but I have never been lead counsel. I don't know if I am ready. I think I am. I prepared everything for the lead counsel on the last two cases and he followed all my suggestions – but maybe that is just because he was sort of busy on other things and just took my suggestions because they were there. Of course, I did fill in for a week as lead counsel a couple of years ago when the primary attorney got ill in the middle of trial, but then he came back and I was so relieved. I just don't know if I can do this.

The man: I have second chaired a number of these cases, but I have never been lead counsel. Of course, I should have been and there is no question that I couldn't have been pretty darn good, given that I basically write everything the lead counsel says. There is only so long you can watch. I am ready.

This internal dialogue can unintentionally impact the way these two people present themselves to the potential client and thus how they are perceived by the potential client. The man, who is convinced he is "ready" will talk confidently about his qualifications, while the woman may hedge a little because she hasn't convinced herself that she can do the job. Since tone, word choices, and body language are what the client sees, she may assume the man is better qualified, more able to do the job, and will be a better fit, even though that may not be true.

The same is seen on social media. Men are far more likely to tell everyone about their successes, whilst women often depend on others to mention it for them. Don't leave it to chance. Take control of your own messaging.

Part of risk-taking is being able to talk about yourself confidently and assertively, and conveying a "can do" attitude to the client, a willingness to take on challenges. While there may be instances where you are perfectly suited and have the exact qualifications the client is looking for, more often than not, you will have to convince the client that you can parlay the experiences you do have into what the client needs. And that means you have to self-promote initially within your firm (so you are given opportunities to show what you can do) and then with potential and current clients.

Self-promotion internally

Within the firm, self-promotion comes from talking about your experience and successes to others and being willing to share your victories appropriately with your colleagues, whether it be in person or online. For example, when you see a partner in the hallway and instead of just saying hi, you can engage him in conversation: "Hey Joe, how are you? It has been a long time since I have seen you. That is mostly because I have been super busy working on a difficult deal – first one I have done on my own. But, I am happy to say we got a terrific result. In fact, the client was so happy he retained us for another matter, which is even bigger."

Of course, in the remote working environment, this becomes harder, as you are not seeing people walking down the hall. So, as discussed previously, you have to make those opportunities by inviting conversations and interactions with partners and senior associates. Ask for a Zoom call or a meeting in the office to discuss an issue. Jump on opportunities to attend meetings in the office. Or better yet, suggest an in-person meeting to discuss an issue or strategy for an upcoming matter. Offer to set up a socializing event on Zoom or other platforms with associates and partners. Go into the office two or three times a week. In other professions, folks may be able to work entirely remotely. In the legal industry, that will not work. Not only is presence in the office important for your substantive development, it is also critical to developing and enhancing your reputation. It doesn't have to be every day; but you need to spend some time in an environment where you are interacting with your colleagues in person.

You also must learn to accept compliments from others without any self-deprecation. For example, when a colleague says, "You did a great job on that matter," do not say, "Oh, it really isn't that big of a deal and besides, I had a talented team that really made this possible". Instead, tweak it ever so slightly and say, "Thank you. I was happy to be able to lead our team of terrific lawyers to this victory." So you accept the compliment, assert your leadership, and acknowledge the contributions of the team. Other ways to self-promote within the firm include asking for opportunities that will help you grow. This means you go to a senior partner who is staffing an important matter and ask to be part of his team. In asking, you talk about the skill set you have and how this experience of working with the senior partner would allow you to enhance those skills and learn from him. You can also ask a senior partner out to lunch to "pick his brain" on how you can increase your business development opportunities, enhance your skill set, and raise your profile within the firm, while telling him that you want to be a partner someday.

Here are some "risks" you can take immediately to raise your visibility internally:

- Seek out and accept stretch assignments.
- Connect with your colleagues on social media, such as LinkedIn, so they see what you are up to regularly.
- Ask for opportunities to be involved in important cases, pitches, and client relationships.
- Volunteer to write blogs and speeches or run webinars with a senior partner.
- Ask a person senior to you out to lunch or coffee.
- Volunteer to work on a pro bono matter being supervised by a rainmaker.
- Get involved in planning events, in person or online, for your practice group – make yourself visible in your firm.

The more visibility you have in the firm, the more you learn from those senior to you and the better chance you have to grow and develop. Staying in your office and doing work that you know you can do may feel good, but it does nothing to build your skill set. Take the risk and seek out opportunities that are outside of your comfort zone.

Self-promotion externally

One way to self-promote with potential clients is to find the common ground between your experience and what the client is looking for. To do this, you may have to think about your experience broadly. For example, let's say a client is looking for someone to handle a fraud claim that she believes will go to trial. You have never taken a fraud claim to trial. But you have tried cases involving other tort claims with similar damages, and you have handled fraud cases that have been resolved short of trial.

Use that experience to sell yourself for this case. So, instead of saying you have never tried a fraud claim, your pitch is that you fully understand fraud claims because they are frequently alleged, you have dealt with fraud claims many times and, while you haven't actually tried a fraud case (because you have settled all of them), you have tried cases involving the kinds of damages this plaintiff is seeking. You should also note, assuming it is true, that the strength of your team lies in strategically positioning the case for summary judgment or settlement, perhaps making the lack of experience actually trying a similar case less important.

You also have to get comfortable talking about your successes and experiences with clients and potential clients in casual meetings and encounters. This doesn't mean you say, "I am the best trial lawyer you can get," or "I win all my cases", but rather that you find a way to work your track record into the conversation. For example, if you were having lunch with a client and she started telling you about an antitrust matter that is making her crazy, you can say, "I know exactly what you mean. I had a case like the one you are describing and here is what happened." By making this part of the conversation, you aren't perceived as saying, "Look at me! Look at me!" but rather you are sharing common ground with the client and, by doing so, demonstrating your expertise and experience. In the same way, if you write a post on LinkedIn describing a recent success, you can refer to the support you had from the rest of the team and how much it meant to you. The point is made. You were successful.

One common way to introduce work-related issues into a casual conversation with an in-house person is to say something like, "So what is keeping you up at night these days?" Or, if you are familiar with what is happening in the industry, you use that to start a conversation with the potential client: "Boy, there is a lot of press lately about harassment claims in tech companies. And a lot of our clients are concerned about this issue. So I am spending a lot of time working on training and preventive measures with them. How is your team handling this issue?" In this short exchange you have demonstrated familiarity with a major issue for the industry, you have mentioned your experience, you have noted an approach to preventing these claims, and you have asked the client to engage on the issue. But, you have never directly asked for business.

I have mentioned earlier that we all have the common experience of the pandemic. Use this to connect with current clients and to use in conversations with potential clients. The universal challenges we all faced during this time provide a baseline for us all. Talking about it makes us relatable and approachable. However, this is not group therapy time; it is simply a way to connect on an issue that everyone has experience and opinions!

The easier part

It goes without saying that you must stand out from the crowd to be a rainmaker. You have to be memorable – perhaps because of your reputation, but more likely because you can demonstrate value in a way that others do not. That means you must distinguish yourself from your competitors.

So, if you are pitching a case, do something that is going to distinguish your team from the other lawyers who are pitching for the same case.

Here is an example. We were asked to pitch a case that was filed in the Midwest. We were a San Francisco firm, so we were going up against local firms that were known to the client. We had two challenges. First, we had to be relatable and not look like some hot shot lawyers coming into town. Second, we had to differentiate ourselves from the other firms. So here is what we did.

First, we took the entire team to the pitch – one partner and two associates. We made sure everyone had a speaking role and we let the client see how we interacted with each other. We joked around, played off each other, and demonstrated our true affection for each other and our passion for what we do.

Secondly, we used social media to research each of their people at the pitch so we could relate to them as individuals. We showed that we had made the effort to find out about them and their careers. We dropped pieces of information into the discussion and the pleasantries at the start of the meeting.

I asked one of the associates – who was one of the smartest lawyers in my group at the time – to come up with a unique theory or strategic move that was "out of the box". He did. He came up with a theory on how we might argue that punitive damages should not be allowed in this case. This was important because the primary exposure to the client was the punitive damage claim.

Here's the secret. Neither he nor I thought the theory would ultimately be accepted by the court. But it wasn't entirely frivolous and it would give the opposing side pause, which might open the door to an early settlement. We decided that this would be important to share with the client so that he could see how we think and how we are always looking to minimize exposure.

I let the associate present this idea to the client during the pitch meeting. The client was quite intrigued, asked a lot of questions, and seemed genuinely impressed by the suggestion.

We left. Two days later we found out we didn't get the case.

So, I took another risk. I called the client and said, "We were very disappointed that we were not selected for this matter and would love your feedback on any ways in which we might improve our presentation next time so that we have a chance of being selected". The client responded that he had decided to go with a local firm because of the judge involved. But then he asked another question, which was this: "Did you really think that punitive damage argument would work?"

I replied honestly and said no, but indicated that I thought it was worth making and that it reflected how we approach our cases – always looking for an argument or an angle that will advance the client's interests. He said he agreed that the argument was probably not viable in the long run, but expressed his appreciation for our willingness to think out of the box.

Two years later, this same client had a matter in California. We were the first and only firm he called. He said he liked our willingness to take risks in our approach to litigating matters. It is the rainmaker's ability to convey expertise, creative thinking, and risk-taking that helps them bring in clients.

> *"If I am not retained by a potential client, I continue to engage with them to find out why I didn't get the business and formulate new and creative approaches when future business opportunities arise."*
>
> Roberta D. Liebenberg, partner, Fine, Kaplan and Black, RPC

> *"As a general counsel, my priorities in selecting outside counsel included diversity, efficiency, good judgment, and, most importantly, a reasonable risk tolerance. Outside lawyers embracing all of these became my most trusted partners."*
>
> Michelle Banks, former general counsel, Gap Inc.

Finding a way to differentiate yourself at a pitch involves risk-taking because you will have to do things that are not "normal". Here are some things I have done at pitches that helped me win new clients:

- Having a PowerPoint presentation, about why we were the right choice for the matter, that had no words – only pictures.
- Not bringing a PowerPoint or any glossy materials at all to hand out.
- Providing the potential client with alternative strategies to approach the matter, some of which are uncommon and risky.
- Brainstorming with the client at the pitch on alternatives to the traditional approach to the litigation or deal.

- Providing concrete examples of our expertise by telling a few good and relevant war stories.
- Giving examples of where I have used innovation and creative approaches at trials or in settlement to achieve the business objectives of the client.
- Giving the client insight into how you work and how you interact with your colleagues by bringing the entire team to the pitch and making sure that each person has a speaking role. This shows the client how you work as a team with your colleagues and gives the client a feel for how you work.
- Using a lot of humor and personal tidbits, as appropriate, to let my true self and that of my team shine. Interactions that show this "non-lawyer" side of you and your team are, more often than not, seen as positives by the client.
- Connecting with them beforehand via LinkedIn to tell them how much I was looking forward to meeting with them and to comment on interesting points in their work or career.
- Sending them blogs, posts, links to webinars, etc. that I have produced on similar issues in advance of the meeting. It appears helpful and demonstrates knowledge and understanding.

While I am citing examples of how I try to differentiate my team in formal pitches, this type of differentiation is necessary in any setting – a lunch or dinner with a potential client or even a networking event where you work into the conversation some information about why your firm or your approach is different from other firms. Differentiation is all about showing strategic thinking, creativity, and innovative approaches. And doing that involves taking risks. The willingness and ability to take risks is what distinguishes a rainmaker from other lawyers.

References

1 "Why women don't apply for jobs unless they're 100 percent qualified," Tara Sophia Mohr, *Harvard Business Review*, 25 August 2014.

Chapter 9: Finding business

Despite what you hear, there are plenty of opportunities to develop new business. The first and most obvious place is existing clients within your firm. This is the low-hanging fruit, but it involves self-promotion, as discussed above, and a willingness to take risks.

> *"When a general counsel asked whether a more experienced partner was available for a meeting with top executives on an important matter, I asked the general counsel whether there was a concern about my ability or a perceived need for a 'gray-haired partner'. The general counsel said, 'The latter'. I told him I could handle it, and I did... [and] was thereafter retained to handle virtually all of their high-profile employment cases."*
>
> Tim Long, shareholder, Greenberg Taurig LLP

The low-hanging fruit: existing clients

Most firms have a certain number of institutional clients. These are clients that have been with the firm for a long time and give a lot of business to the firm. There are many ways to break into these clients. Here are a few examples of how you might do this.

Volunteer to work on matters for the institutional client. This means you go to the partner who controls the business and – take a risk – offer to work on a case or matter. You might say, for example, "I hear you just got a new matter in for Company X. I have always been interested in doing some work for that company. So if there is any way I could help, let me know." If there is not an opportunity to work on a particular matter, make sure the relationship partner knows you are interested in being considered for the next matter.

Assuming you get to work on a matter from an institutional client, make sure you also talk directly to the junior employees of that client. As discussed above, these folks are the future and you want to have a good relationship with them. They may also leave and go to another client and, if so, you want to be the one they call from their new company. Court them by interacting with them – invite them to lunch, make periodic "How are you?" calls, look for opportunities to showcase them at conferences or other public places, tag them on social media and sing their praises to their bosses. Note: You may want to advise the relationship partner of your intent to connect with this person so he or she is not caught off guard by finding out about it from the client. This also shows the partner that you understand the importance of building relationships up and down the client's chain of command, which should be viewed as a good thing.

Another opportunity exists when there is an institutional client who does not use your practice group. In this instance, you might want to find a way to get introduced to the client so that you can pitch your practice group or do introduce your practice group to the client by doing a CLE program for him. In most firms, you must start by going to the person who controls the client. Note: you should not go directly to the client. Rather, you advise the relationship partner that you would like to do this, and then you gather information from the relationship partner about the client, including why they aren't using your practice group, who they are using for that work, and what the chances are of getting them to consider switching to you.

There are several dynamics to consider here, however. First, you do not want to threaten the relationship partner in any way – to make him or her feel that you are trying to make a move on this client. Second, the client may have a good reason for not using your practice group – e.g. she likes diversification of law firms, she gets a better price from another firm, she came from the firm she is using and feels loyalty to them. You need that information before you can decide if this is a viable move. Once you have that information, you strategize with the relationship partner as to the best way to get in front of the client, or not.

If you are working with an institutional client, you can also ask that client to introduce you to other institutions that are in a similar industry or have similar legal issues. Again, however, particularly if you are a junior partner or senior associate, you need to be sensitive to the relationship partner and make sure you are not stepping on his/her toes in any way by making that type of request.

Friends who can give out business

Asking a friend for business may feel like a bridge too far for some people and, thus, may be a non-starter. And while I hate to make a gender stereotype, I think that is truer for women than for men. In fact, it is not uncommon for men to be on the golf course or at a sporting event and to say to a friend who is a potential client, "So why the heck aren't we doing your work?" Women, for the most part, don't do that. Why? Many women will say that it feels like it jeopardizes the friendship or seems inappropriate.

But my advice to anyone with this hesitation is this: get over it. Friends can be a great source of new business. Asking is not that hard. Imagine you are at a swim meet with your friend who is the general counsel of a large company. She shares in the chit chat that takes place between events that she has been super busy because her company is facing a difficult legal issue that is right up your alley. That is a golden opportunity that shouldn't be wasted. You are a trusted advisor to her as her friend. So you can say, "Hey, this is something I deal with all the time. Let me tell you how I would approach it." You can even offer to look at what she is doing for free. You don't ask for the business. You simply let her know that you are an expert, a resource, and available to her. And then you see what happens. Think of it this way. Many times you are an advisor for your friend on non-business issues – how to deal with teenagers, where to shop for comfortable shoes, a golf course open at twilight with discounted rates, whatever. You are a source of information and they trust your advice. So why would you deny them your expertise and experience on issues relating to their business?

There is another group of "friends" you should court. These are people who went to college and law school with you. They may not be close friends, but they are resources for potential business. In fact, as you enter your late 30s and early 40s, many of these "friends" will be in-house as lawyers or businesspeople and may have the ability to give out business. Social media provides easy access to this group of people and it is worth the time to track them down and open communications again if you don't already have them as a connection. Message them after a while and ask them if they would like to meet up. Of course, you aren't going to start out asking for business; that comes later, but they should have a good idea of your specialisms and experience from your social media posts and online profile.

Never say "never" to networking

You have many sources from which potential clients may come. These include your personal and online networks, attorneys within your firm, leads generated by firm events and webinars, and arising from bar activities and community involvement. All of these groups can be great sources for business. So, use every opportunity that comes your way to put yourself out there.

The key to networking is feeling comfortable. To do that, you are going to have to develop your own personal style – you can't just copy what someone else does. And, while for some attorneys the whole idea of networking seems daunting, for most of us it is just a matter of finding some tools and strategies that work for you. Here are some that I have found useful:

- Try to identify in advance who is going to be at a networking event and choose two or three of these people to seek out for a conversation.
- Do some internet research on these people – don't stalk them, but find out a little about them other than their names.
- Think about a few things that you can bring up at the event that are relevant to the person or his job. These don't have to be business related; they can be social issues – you know the person likes food so you have a new restaurant to discuss; you know the person has kids who just started pre-school so you put that on the list of things to speak with him about; you know his company was just acquired so you ask about the status of that. Once you put your mind to it, you will find many things of common interest. Follow the adage, however – stay away from politics.
- Determine in advance what you want out of this encounter: a commitment for lunch or drinks; a follow-up phone call; an opportunity to send this person some materials; or simply a connection.
- If you don't know in advance who is going to be at the event, walk up to groups of people and introduce yourself. Then activate your active listening skills and find ways to interact – by asking questions or offering comments. (I have to credit my mom for getting me comfortable with this approach. I loved running for office when I was in school and I was pretty successful at it, but in my first attempts to run for a school-wide office in my 2,000-student junior high school, my mom told me I had to just walk up to people, introduce myself, and say I was running for office. You can imagine how horrifying this seemed to an already overly self-conscious teenager. But my mom was relentless. So I tried it and it worked – for the most part. My message? If a junior high school kid can do this, with few developed social skills, so can you.)
- Have an exit strategy. If you feel the conversation topics are limited, then say at the appropriate time: "It was so nice talking with you,

but I don't want to monopolize all your time! [Insert the ask – "I will give you a call about lunch" or "Here is my card, let's keep in touch", etc.] Thanks!"

- Be sure to have cards and get cards. In fact, I like to get cards from everyone I meet at a networking event so that when I get back to my office I can send emails to all of them, personalizing those emails appropriately for the people I really want to continue to work on for potential business. ("Loved our conversation; would you be up for doing lunch sometime so we can continue to chat?" or "So enjoyed speaking with you. Sounds like you are facing some interesting challenges at work. Let's talk because now that I have had some time to think, I have some ideas for you.") You can also connect on social media. It gives you another opportunity to connect and perhaps point out a relevant post to them.
- Follow up. If you say you are going to send something, or call about getting together, do it. (And by the way, agreeing to send someone something after an encounter at a networking event is a terrific way to have a second "touch" with that person.)

Other sources of networking

You need to network within your firm and externally. As discussed above, firm networking usually consists of raising your visibility by taking opportunities to have interactions with people who have business and/or are working on matters that will allow you to increase your opportunities to go on pitches, meet institutional clients, and assume lead roles on cases and deals. This is critical to your success, as your internal reputation sets you up for future business.

Also, most firms run various types of "training" for clients – where clients are invited to the firm for a morning or afternoon seminar/webinar on the latest "new thing". Volunteer to be part of those events in whatever way you can. Find out which clients are coming and plan who you want to meet. Invite people you know who are not firm clients to come to the event. Write something for the event and get it published, or ask for a speaking role at the event.

There are also several types of external events available for networking. This includes everything from ABA and state bar association events to conferences. At these events, you have the opportunity to meet attorneys from all over the country. Use these events to practice your networking skills, but also to make contact with people who might be able to give you or your firm business. But don't limit yourself to lawyer-dominated events. As discussed in more detail below, track and think about attending industry events where you will have the opportunity to meet business-people and in-house lawyers.

Cold calls can work, sometimes

Cold calls are the most difficult type of business development. To be successful at this, you should develop a strategy and an approach that makes sense and feels comfortable to you. You also must be sure to comply with any ethical restrictions that might apply. But cold calls can be effective.

One of the easiest methods for cold calling is to use industry or subject matter expertise you have developed as the hook for approaching a potential client. For example, if you have just advanced a creative or innovative legal theory or argument successfully, you might want to seek out speaking opportunities to discuss how you accomplished this and what it means to clients. From my days as in-house at Bank of America where we did all of our litigation ourselves, I developed an expertise in the National Bank Act defense to employment claims. This was a fairly obscure and seldom used defense at the time. When I left the Bank to go to a private firm, I sought out opportunities to talk about the defense to organizations like the California Bankers Association and the American Bankers Association. From those opportunities, I got work from several banks whose outside counsel had never used or understood the power of this defense.

Another option is to have your firm host an event where current clients and potential clients are invited to hear about a development you've been working on. If you meet someone at a networking event and they express an interest in an area where you have expertise, offer (at the appropriate time, which is probably not at the networking event) to do a CLE presentation on the subject to the in-house lawyers.

Since the use of digital email marketing has become more widespread, many believe they can avoid picking up the phone to potential contacts and simply leave it to emails. At some point those emails do have to develop into personal contact in order to secure work, but at least you know that if that contact is responding to emails or webinar invitations they are genuinely interested. That makes contacting them a lot easier than walking into a room of new people and trying to guess where to start.

There are numerous ways, including various social media sites, to get information about yourself to potential clients. You can contribute to websites or write something for a well-read blog or an industry publication. There are many magazines, podcasts, and journals that are geared to particular industries. Think about using those avenues to build your reputation in the industry and as an entrée to a cold call on clients in that industry. This all takes effort on your part and thinking out of the box. However, if you can get them interested in hearing more, you now can make a call that may get you some business.

You may also want to identify an industry in which you have expertise and attend industry meetings or trade shows – in part to learn the business and in part to network with people attending. You can also write blogs on social media or for your own website, aimed at that industry or that trade show, and use relevant keywords or hashtags so your content appears in front of the right people on search engine lists or in their social feed. Similarly, you might think about joining groups that don't have a lot of lawyers, where you might be able to get on a program to speak about a subject of interest to them. For example, there are industry conferences that address employment, antitrust, cybersecurity, advertising, financial issues, etc., where you could be on a panel or be a speaker. How do you get those opportunities? Through research and by asking your existing clients what kinds of industry events they attend and then asking them to help you get on a program.

There are a lot of clients looking for attorneys. Simply identifying businesses you would like to represent, doing research on their legal footprint and who they use for legal advice, identifying some critical issues on which you are an expert, and trying to get in front of a decision maker is still a valid route to a potential client. I wouldn't expect a lot of bang for your buck here, as these are the most difficult kinds of business development issues. But, perhaps, you might want to take a risk and try it at least once. I know of one firm that developed a swat team of their best rainmakers and gave them a list of potential clients. While they were only able to meet with about 40 percent of the clients on the list, they eventually got some business out of these cold calls and, of course, expanded the reputation of their firm, which might inure to their benefit in the future.

And while the types of efforts described above to elevate your cold calling opportunities are not the most efficient way to get those clients, it can't hurt because it builds your brand and builds your reputation. It is risky, therefore, on several levels, but with big risk comes big rewards.

Chapter 10: The inevitability of digital for the rainmaker

By Rebecca Harding, Saltwhistle Communications

Today, having an online presence is inevitable. You might not want one. You might not have actively created one. But you will have one in any case. It is impossible to carry on in today's world without somebody, somewhere, writing something about you. Even if it's simply on your own firm's website.

The problem is that if you don't take control of that profile then it can run wild. If you are going out to build relationships and win work, you need to know what impression of you people are getting. That online profile is the context within which you work and establish relationships.

And then there is the competition. If you're not present online, somebody else will be. They will be the one creating the relationships. They will be the one generating new contacts. They will be the one benefiting from the work. To be quite honest, you simply don't have a choice but to get yourself online if you want to build your reputation and establish professional relationships on the back of it.

All your clients will be online too, particularly if they are businesspeople. They will look at your online presence and compare it with their own, as well as comparing it to other lawyers and advisors. They will make a judgment about your professionalism, how up-to-date your legal advice is, and how active you are in the marketplace based on your online presence. You need to make sure they are getting the right impression.

The internet has made the market even more competitive than it was before. Professionals no longer restrict themselves geographically and their clients don't either. Now we can hire people we've never even met in person. We can work together online, so developing a digital relationship is crucial. I would say that 90 percent of my current work has been generated through relationships initially built online, and 50 percent of my current clients live internationally. You can build good interpersonal relationships by spending time chatting online, emailing, and following all the same rules to generate loyalty and trust in those relationships as mentioned elsewhere in this book. Any true rainmaker will be front and center when it comes to digital content.

Does it really help win business?

Over recent years there has been a complete overhaul of how clients and potential clients look for their professionals. Today they conduct their own research, rather than relying purely on referral, and will base their decisions to a large degree on the online presence that they see.

Forrester[1] conducted research and found that potential clients gather information from at least three sources to reinforce their decision before they instruct someone as their lawyer. The most important sources of research they use are as follows:

- 30 percent like to hear you speak.
- 20 percent read blogs and articles that you have written.
- 17 percent have had some interaction with you on social media.
- 15 percent would read a book that you've written, even if it is a handbook or an e-book of some sort.
- Eight percent will look at your website and make a judgment.
- Five percent will look at online reviews.
- Five percent will do an online search.

You need to be sure that you feature and that the messages you are giving about yourself are consistent across all of them. One of the first things that I always recommend to people is that they do a Google search on themselves and see what comes up. It can be enlightening.

Building digital relationships can help overcome the problems that online working patterns present when you are used to old fashioned, face-to-face meetings. You may have begun the connection on an email or a "like" on a social media platform, but eventually you will talk face-to-face, even if it is via a phone or a computer screen. You can still engage in all the same relationship-building activities, e.g. offering clients opportunities to attend events that might be of interest, introducing them to useful contacts, trying to promote their businesses, etc. All of these activities will build loyalty for you and will increase the chances of that client, or target, selecting you to work with.

Professionals always try to justify their decisions with rational arguments and business reasoning. The reality is that people make decisions based on their emotions. Nobel Prize winner Daniel Kahneman undertook research[2] on how people make decisions. He revealed that our brains have two distinct operating systems – System 1 and System 2.

- System 1 is based on fast, instinctive, unconscious, and emotional factors. Generally, it is thought to account for over 90 percent of all decision-making, including decisions made in business situations.
- System 2 is based on rational thinking and deliberate logic. This accounts for only a small proportion of all decisions made. A far cry from what we would believe is true as professionals!

As long as we can keep building loyalty and generating an emotional response from people, even if it is online, we stand a very good chance of developing relationships that will bear fruit in terms of work and long-term connections. So, yes, it works in exactly the same way.

Advantages of connecting online

One of the advantages of connecting online is the ability to monitor who is "liking" and "sharing" particular content on certain topics. In the case of email mass mailings, if you invest in some tracking software, you should be able to see who is genuinely interested in your content by their online activity, such as reading your material and visits to your profile pages. For someone who has spent hours at sometimes fruitless networking events, hoping that at some point you will encounter a person that may prove to be a helpful, long-term contact, the idea of being able to see immediately those who are genuinely interested in what you do is thrilling. Not only can you see what they are interested in, but you can contact them and initiate the conversation with the guaranteed knowledge that they will be receptive to the relationship. You already know what's concerning them because of what you can see in their online activity. You know how to start the conversation. You know they have a problem. You are already more than halfway there thanks to digital relationship building, your online presence, and a bit of smart tracking code.

Social media policy

Before you start in earnest, it's always worth checking whether your firm has a social media policy. It's important to know what the firm's stance is on social media, and have a clear understanding of what you can and cannot do in your own name. There are often blurry edges between your own profile and the profile of your firm.

Building your personal brand

As mentioned earlier, it is important to decide what it is that you stand for and the messages that you want people to take away about you. The great thing about social media is that it allows you to establish this reputation in the marketplace with connections that you haven't met yet, as well as with those you do. You can show them the kind of work you do, your attitude to your clients and your team, and you can demonstrate original thinking and creativity. You can talk about your successes. You can establish the structure of your personal "brand".

Titles

Professional titles are valuable. They encourage people to respond to you and gain online recognition. To stand out online it is useful to have a title of some sort that will attract attention and drive people to connect with you. It does not always have to be a legal title. It can be chairman of a committee within one of your target market groups. For example, if you are targeting dentists, then being on a committee within their professional association would help you establish more contacts in the medical sphere. Such a title gives you credibility and status that your firm title alone does not. You are seen as more authoritative and neutral. Your contact is viewed as a networking advantage. In terms of generating digital connections, and ultimately work, anything that makes you stand out from the background clamor is a good thing.

Tribes

You have probably heard of the term "tribe" to describe distinct groups of digital followers. Building your tribe simply means building an online community that has the same interests and motivations as yourself. In a world where true differential as a professional is difficult to achieve (as said before, we are all technically excellent and trusted advisors), building a tribe for yourself can be the way to do it. One lawyer I know in Canada chose to talk openly about her commitment to the movement against the testing of makeup and toiletries on animals. She built up a strong following of businesses and organizations, and more particularly, individuals within those organizations, who agreed with her sentiments. Some might baulk at this rather politicized approach and think this was a risky strategy, but in actual fact what it did was create hard-core loyalty amongst a number of businesspeople who were personally, and professionally, committed to what she was trying to achieve.

As a result, she won more work than she ever had before in her career.

She used digital platforms to increase her personal "reach" and "range" of influence as well as connecting and building her network. She showed originality in her content – her message – and as a result was rewarded by loyalty from those she attracted, and ultimately by work.

She differentiated herself in the marketplace, but not in the traditional way. She showed herself to be committed to a cause, thereby presenting her own personality. She was respected for that. This began online, but soon flowed into the real world too.

Understanding how it works

Despite using digital platforms widely to promote themselves and their firms, many lawyers are unclear as to how different digital platforms integrate to establish reputation and build relationships. A rainmaker will adopt a cohesive approach and see no boundaries between online and in-person relationship building. There should be a good flow of interaction and contact between the two.

Figure 1 overleaf shows how each of the common marketing activities that most lawyers engage in are used at different times in the process of building relationships with prospective clients. These go on in the background and reinforce any real-world contact that takes place.

Ultimately, it is designed to develop a relationship to the point where you transfer the contact from an electronic basis to a real one. A digital exchange is not a replacement for a personal relationship.

Some professionals like getting to know someone without ever having personal contact and use digital as a way to avoid it. The thing to remember is that you are likely to get a good reception if you make the move. From their perspective, they will know you, they will know your work areas, they will know the sort of person you are because they've seen you, and they will feel that you are familiar – all from your digital activity. This means they will be more open to that initial conversation with you. Half the work is already done. It makes your life a lot easier.

In order to understand how digital works it is important to understand the journey that you are taking your potential client on when you are trying to win work. Firstly, you have to build awareness that you exist and then you want them to consider and evaluate your skill base. After a greater level of contact with you, they may then consider buying from you.

Their ongoing relationship with you builds a grounding of good "client experiences", which leads to long-term loyalty. For example, inviting them and their families to events as described earlier. The diagram shows the stages of relationship development and the kind of activities that would take place at different points in that journey. It is a journey you take with your client as a rainmaker.

If you can plot where your client is on this relationship development map then you can start to decide what you need to do next to further that relationship.

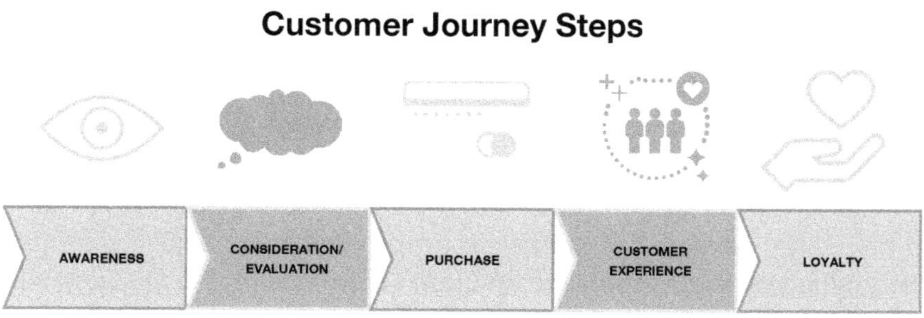

1. Phase: AWARENESS: The user is becoming aware of a product.
2. Phase: CONSIDERATION & EVALUATION: The user is actively looking for information, reviews and options or comparable products.
3. Phase: PURCHASE: The user is ready to buy.
4. Phase: CUSTOMER EXPERIENCE: The user has an experience with the product or solution.
5. Phase: LOYALTY: The user becomes a loyal Brand Advocate.

Figure 1: The stages of relationship development.

Which platforms?

Many people wonder which platforms they should be seen on and how to start their digital adventure. The bottom line is you need to go where your clients are. These platforms may be digital, but it's no different to any other form of communication. You wouldn't choose to write an article for a sewing magazine if you were trying to reach real estate agents.

Social media changes very quickly and the platforms are constantly introducing new initiatives to try and keep up with one another. Who knows which new platform is around the corner? Social media will continue to change and smart businesses and clever individuals will make sure that they are everywhere. Many well thought of international consultancies have accounts on every channel, so don't rule any out.

These days this is very easy to achieve. There are many platforms that will allow you to post content on all your social media accounts at the same time. In other words, you create one post on the software and it sends it out to, for example, Facebook, Instagram, LinkedIn, and Twitter, all at the same time. The other advantage of these platforms is that you can schedule your posts over a longer period of time. You can reduce a month's worth of content into an hour or so's work and scheduling activity. This makes life much easier.

However, you still need to spend time each day replying to comments, and "liking" and "sharing" other people's posts in order to grow relationships and build your online network. Otherwise, you're just sending information out rather than building relationships or actively listening.

Active listening

Just as in real life, a rainmaker will listen carefully to potential clients as they talk about their problems, concerns, and interests, as well as engaging with them on a personal level, so they will do this online too. Obviously the form this takes is slightly different. Any of the following will help enhance your relationship with someone online and engage with them:

- Like their posts regularly and comment on them.
- Share their posts and comment with praise or acknowledgement of their expertise. They will be grateful to you for this as they will have online targets too.
- Make online introductions within messaging apps.
- Post blogs on particular topics and tag particular contacts to ask what they think.
- Start a Facebook group for contacts with similar issues with you as the administrator.
- Respond to comments on your posts.
- Ask questions and encourage a response.
- Ask for feedback or advice.

Consistency

There are two aspects to online consistency – regularity and consistent messaging. Whether you are making contact with potential clients or existing clients online or in person, it's essential that you are consistent, not only about your personal brand messaging, but also in terms of the regularity of the contact. Digital works because of something called "Opportunities To See" (OTS). This is an advertising term and means that people start to recognize a brand or a message because they have had so many opportunities to see it through different channels. The more they see you, and the more contact they have with you, the more familiar you will become. You want to achieve a situation, as said before, where you become a well-known name to them, so when they come across you they can say, "Oh yes! I've heard of you."

Integrations

If you're serious about growing clients through your online presence then integration of your online and real-world activities is necessary. This isn't only to ensure a consistent brand and messaging. It is a case of ensuring that you are making the most of your time and using one idea to its maximum.

If you come up with something smart and innovative, make the most of it. For example, if you produce a podcast on a particular topic, you can then turn this idea into a blog article, you can post it on social media to promote it, you can email out to clients and targets to encourage people to listen. You can send personal emails to close contacts to encourage them to listen to it too.

One piece of content can give you multiple opportunities to build relationships and turn your expertise and thinking into a diverse resource.

If you do this consistently it will generate conversations and ultimately work.

Attracting new contacts

If you want to attract new clients and contacts online then you will need to work smart. There has to be something attractive about you to make them want to connect.

Content

If a rainmaker is thinking in the right way, they will be producing original content that is different to what everyone else is producing – i.e. practical, aimed at business, and recognizing the needs of the client because they listen.

The reality is that the majority of what we see online is just a regurgitation of what everyone else is saying. You rarely see original thinking in blogs and posts. Those that do take a risk and produce something that is perhaps funny, imaginative, and still has a core of technical expertise, will attract far more attention and more followers.

Hashtags

When you are posting online, always think about including a hashtag. A hashtag is simply a word or phrase preceded by # and used on social media, websites, and applications to identify digital content on a specific topic, for example #Rainmaker.

Search engines and platforms aggregate all the content with that same hashtag, making it easier for people to discover posts around specific topics. If someone is interested in that topic they are likely to see your post. This way you can generate brand-new connections and attract people who are genuinely interested in the topics that you are talking about.

Write that book

Forrester showed us that people like to read a book that we've written. It creates professional authority in a subject. With the ability to produce PDF books/e-books or to publish ourselves through online publishing platforms, producing our own book is now as easy as ABC (although it's always advisable to get a professional editor, no matter how good we think we are at writing!).

If the book is designed to help your target market it will establish you as an authority in that area and make a great gift for clients, and potential clients, when building relationships. People are far more likely to hire you to work on a particular job if you're the person that wrote the book about it. The bottom line is a book will start the conversation for you.

Online profiles/bios

You need to have developed a good collection of online profiles/bios for different uses. The number of profiles that you see that are incomplete, have no photograph, don't have a job description, have mistakes, and are poorly laid out continues to amaze me. It is no different to turning up at an event having not bothered to get dressed properly and having badly printed business cards with spelling mistakes on them. People will judge your professionalism these days from your online profile. In fact, it's the first place most people look to find out about you before they meet you. Therefore, you need to take as much care over your online profiles as you would over the profile for your firm's website.

If you find it difficult to write your own profile and to demonstrate your successes, it is often easier to write it in the third person, as though someone has written it for you. It can take away some of those uncomfortable feelings that we sometimes experience when focusing on ourselves.

On a platform like LinkedIn, you can also see who is looking at your profile. I find this a great way of making new connections as they are clearly interested in me already as they have taken a look. I ask them if there's any reason why they read my profile and comment positively on their profiles. These questions can initiate conversations, which then lead to further follow-up. I once did this and connected with a businessman who not only gave me a great piece of work, but also connected me to many other people, who then went on to give me further work. He has proven to be the most valuable contact I have ever made professionally.

Make the first move

You can go on to connect with more people. This is similar to the cold calling discussed before. If you can find an area where you have an interest, school, a previous employer, or some other point of reference in common, it is easy to make a new connection. What people don't like as much is cold calls that are not personalized, whether it is by email or social media. The important thing is to make people feel valued and that you're genuinely interested in them as an individual. It does not change whether that is done in person or via digital means.

Don't be afraid to contact people and ask them to connect with you. There is usually an option to send people a quick note if you're asking to connect and this is a good idea, particularly if you can demonstrate that you have read their profile properly and mention something in it.

The first hundred contacts are always the hardest to obtain and it's a good idea to start with people that you know. The algorithms on the platform will then start to suggest other people that you might know. People are far more likely to connect with you if they see that you know someone else they know. You can quickly start to expand your network.

Belong to you

Ultimately, every contact you make online belongs to you. If you choose to move firms, those contacts go with you. So do the relationships and, you would hope, eventually the work.

I'm not sure that firms have really thought this through. One client's old firm paid a contractor to generate some fantastic LinkedIn leads for a particular service area. As there was some confusion as to where these leads would land, they ended up being connected to her personal LinkedIn profile. A little while later she moved firms and subsequently took all of those contacts with her. I'm not sure anyone even remembered at the original firm. But the value of those contacts was tremendous in terms of relationship-building in the long-term and potential work. Far greater than the size of the bill paid to the contractor!

Live streaming and webinars

We saw earlier that 30 percent of potential clients like to see you speak before instructing you. You are now able to reach a much wider audience, over a larger geographical area, without even moving from your home. Webinars and online conferences have opened up the "speaking" marketplace to everyone. There are now far more opportunities to get in front of a new audience through your contacts or those of other colleagues.

Many platforms now give you the option of live streaming or running webinars and events through them. This is a great way of increasing your network and allowing people to see you in person whilst demonstrating your knowledge, personality, and skills.

If you advertise your event widely via social media and ask your colleagues and friends to share details, you can build up contacts quickly and you will be sure of the areas of law that are an issue for them and where to open the conversation with them. The key is to choose your topic matter wisely and attract your audience.

Once people have attended your event, be quick to connect with them via the messaging part of the app, or by email, and you can begin to build a more personal relationship with those attendees. Many people fall into the trap of only using email automation and scheduled responses to contact people. If you're talking large numbers this works to a certain degree, but if you pick your targets carefully and make the effort to do a personal message or suggest a coffee, you can make far more progress, and they will appreciate it more. This comes back to listening and two-way communication.

The most effective time to contact people directly is immediately after the webinar. In my experience, they are so pleased that you've got in touch with them that they will tell you a great deal about their own current business situation or the issues that are affecting them.

This is the moment when you are most likely to secure a meeting or a follow-up of some sort. Often, lawyers leave it for several weeks before they contact those attendees and it will never have the same impact as it does in those first moments after they have seen you perform live online.

The bottom line is that being seen personally online almost gives the impression of being on a media such as television. It is subconscious, but people perceive an air of authority. We have all seen the queue at conferences as people wait to talk to the keynote speaker. It's the same thing. Take advantage of the psychological impact the screen has and use that authority and momentary interest to build those relationships.

Online partnerships

Another way to build relationships and connections online is to invite others to join you as your expert guest on webinars, blogs, and podcasts. As well as cementing a relationship with that client, you benefit from two other helpful side effects. Firstly, that person will forward and share whatever it is that you have generated in terms of content. This will put you in front of a whole new audience, and one that you can then start connecting with and generate leads through.

"Association" is your second side effect. By associating yourself with others through activities or even simple photographs, you are seen as sharing their attributes and positive strengths. It is also seen as a recommendation of you by the other person. If they share your joint content with their own networks, that is the equivalent of them recommending you. This is a strong foundation upon which to build new connections within their network. These new people will be receptive and ready to listen.

Testimonials

Online testimonials work in much the same way. They help to build relationships through association. If a connection can see that someone they know has left a good testimonial about you online, they are going to be far more open to you approaching them to connect and following up with a call. Online introductions work the same way.

Moving it to the real world

No matter how wonderful your relationships are online, at some point a rainmaker will move it into the real world. This is the point where many stumble. Picking up the phone and making that call or suggesting that you meet for a coffee is the area where I get asked the most for advice.

As I always say, and it has been said here before, the worst answer you can get is "no". You have nothing to lose.

Some say they'd like to discuss aspects of their career or ask for advice. I say that I'd like to extend my network and that I would enjoy the opportunity to chat with them. I suggest that I can make introductions and can share my connections with them. This is often enough to generate that first coffee or virtual meeting. You have to move the relationship to the next stage. You can't exist online alone.

Make a plan

There are many things to think about in terms of your digital reputation and presence, and its impact on your ability to win work. Why not sit down and work out what you are going to do over the next year? For example, you might want to write a blog, do a voice recording each month, or expand into a range of social media. Whatever you do, keep it up. If you do it regularly, people come to expect it and they will look for it. This is building a relationship. It puts you first and foremost in their mind and that is a good thing when it comes to attributing work. Whatever you plan to do, stick to it.

In the end, it all comes down to implementation. We are only ever as good as what we're prepared to put the time into doing. What you put in, you will get out. If you don't put the time into those people online, somebody else will. And it's never too late to start.

References

1 https://spinsucks.com/entrepreneur/referral-marketing/

2 Daniel Kahneman, *Thinking, Fast and Slow* (Farrar, Straus and Giroux, 2013).

Chapter 11: If you don't believe us...

When the Rainmaking Study came out, I thought it accurately captured what was missing from much of the training that was being done by law firms. While we certainly weren't the first to note that business development was simply "selling" spelled with different letters, our study was unique because we had data available in a readable and understandable format for lawyers to consider.

So, I took the Rainmaking Study on the road, doing countless conferences, bar association meetings, firm retreats, and other types of presentations. The format I used to present the information included a panel discussion with one or two general counsel and two or three rainmakers. And what I discovered was that – without prompting – the characteristics identified in the study were exhibited by the participants on the panels. More importantly, every time we did these panel discussions, the rainmakers would be different – some extreme extroverts, some introverts, and everything in between. But the way they discussed how they built their books of business inevitably came down to the same two fundamentals – reputation and relationships.

Similarly, the general counsel (and senior in-house lawyers who give out work) also mirrored the study's findings of what makes rainmakers successful. Clearly, they care deeply about reputation; but they also want to enjoy working with the people they hire as their lawyers. And that means clients are looking for excellent legal services coupled with some of the softer factors that differentiate those lawyers from their competitors.

Alan Bryan, managing counsel II – commercial litigation, Walmart Stores, Inc., said it this way:

> *"Margaret Mead once said, 'Always remember that you are absolutely unique. Just like everyone else.' Sometimes I think she had lawyers in mind when she said it. I've had the honor to interview hundreds of attorneys who want to work for our company in a variety of areas. One question I often ask is, 'What makes you or your firm unique?' In other words, what should make an attorney managing our matters choose you over counsel*

already being utilized? I can tell you, it's not going to be that 'you're the best' at that subject or that your firm puts 'client service first'. These and other generic descriptors that everyone says get you nowhere. I want to know what knowledge, relationship, skill set, etc. that you or your firm possess will cost-efficiently advance my company's interests or protect our assets. Everyone is the 'best' in the legal profession – what truly makes you unique to our company among the multitude of attorneys who want to do our work?"

A word from the experts

Below, I have included some of the statements from lawyers who have or had the ability to give out business. As you will see, their comments confirm and expand on many of the ideas laid out in this book.

"I looked for the following non-obvious items in lawyers within outside firms when I was GC – a positive connection at first and then a trusted partnership; good judgment; and risk tolerance, which needs to be emphasized and encouraged with lawyers who tend to be averse to it for reasons stemming from the fundamentals of our profession, especially the power of precedent."

Michelle Banks, former general counsel, Gap Inc.

"My outside counsel was a trusted and highly valued partner, both personally and professionally. She not only possessed an incredible understanding of employment law, but also had strong business acumen, with a pragmatic and creative solutions approach. In as much, she clearly understood the needs of the business and the desired business outcome, and instead of using employment law as a barrier, she possessed a unique ability to turn a barrier into an opportunity, resulting in favorable business results. In addition, from a personal perspective, she was a trusted advisor, who was always there for me, a true partner."

Joan Cronin, former head of human resources, various companies

"I look for outside counsel that will make me do my job better. Of course, I want all the normal things like responsiveness, excellent understanding of the subject matter, great writing. But I also want someone who can help me figure out the right practical advice. When I am thinking about who to put on a matter or who to call with a problem, I worry less about getting

a big-name firm and more about the perspective my counsel will bring to my matter. In some cases, this means bringing knowledge from a certain legal community with which I am unfamiliar; in other cases, it means having successfully handled a matter similar to mine or against the same opposing counsel; sometimes it means having specialized knowledge or a creative way of attacking a case. I want something I don't have from my outside counsel, and when someone can show me that they are going to add value and perspective, that is who I want to handle my matter."

Heidi Swartz, vice president, deputy general counsel, employment law and investigations, Facebook

"The outside lawyers I hired when I was general counsel of Lawrence Livermore National Laboratory had to be smart, strategic, and experts in their field. They had to know how to manage litigation efficiently and in a cost-effective manner. All of the teams I brought in to interview for litigation matters had those qualities. The firms I hired, however, were able to show me in the interview process that the lawyers they were presenting to work on my matters operated as a cohesive team, were interested in and would assist us in reaching our business objectives, and would treat me and my team as equal partners in our quest to achieve those objectives."

Jan Tulk, former laboratory counsel (general counsel), Lawrence Livermore National Laboratory

"In hiring outside counsel, some of the key factors we look for are responsiveness, efficiency, and effective communication. Our outside counsel should be willing to listen to our goals and objectives, and should understand our business. We also strongly value diversity."

Naomi Waltman, executive vice president and deputy general counsel, litigation, Paramount Global (f/k/a ViacomCBS Inc.), CBS Corporation

"Hiring outside counsel is among the most important responsibilities of a general counsel. In my experience the hiring decision is driven by two factors – performance, which includes evaluating the firm's talent, the diversity of their teams, and their experience; and culture, which includes trying to evaluate traits like independent thinking and perseverance, and examining the firm's success at succession planning and talent development."

Denise Keane, former executive vice-president and general counsel, Altria Group, Inc.

"Understanding our perspective is essential. For example: Late bills mean, I don't care about your internal financial metrics. Long memos mean, I am really smart, and you are not (and your time isn't that important). Ambivalence means = it's your job on the line, not mine. Surprise means = I am too busy (or unorganized) to keep you advised."

Rachel Giesber Clingman, vice president,
Legal Petroleum & Potash, bhpbilliton

"We expect our outside counsel to provide sound, efficient, and principled counsel and to partner with us in serving the business. 'Sound' gets to the basics: expert counsel, provided in a practical, timely, and thoughtful way. Efficiency is about how that counsel is provided: efficient in terms of cost, staffing, and responsiveness. 'Principled' is a critical component of good counsel and includes respectful, professional, and inclusive service that is keenly mindful of reputational risk, industry practices and developments, conflicts of interest (both for the firm and among parties to a particular matter), and the need to offer diverse perspectives. And lastly, the partnership we seek with our most trusted counsel is one in which the firm will proactively, thoughtfully, and creatively work with us to manage risk and achieve goals. We don't need more blast email alerts; we need the phone call when the latest SEC enforcement action comes down that might somehow implicate practices in our world."

Karyn S. Polak, formerly deputy general counsel,
PNC Bank, National Association

"In choosing outside counsel, I look for someone that I can confidently put in front of the business one day and the Court the next without having to explain that those are different audiences."

Senior litigation counsel for a large tech company

Conclusion

Our "non-lawyer" salespeople friends have always understood that to be effective and successful in business you not only need to have an excellent product, but you must also be able to sell it. Yet, for years, lawyers have thought of business development as an add-on to their day jobs of being excellent lawyers. That is why, in many firms, hours spent on business development are treated differently from billable hours. And yet, there are no billable hours without business development.

So, my goal is to take a cue from the "nons". Let's take the mystery, or the drudgery (depending on how you look at it), out of business development and make it part of everyday life for lawyers. Let's recognize that building client relationships takes more than a checklist or a business plan, more than a good reputation and a good firm. Rainmaking requires that you let your whole self be seen – not just the analytical lawyer. Let the client see you have a sense of humor, a personality, a family; that you can show empathy and that you are relatable. Connect with clients by using your emotional IQ as well as your intellect. Show that you understand that clients have personal lives, career goals, a boss, and their own challenges, by thinking of how you can help them as well as how they can help you.

And enjoy yourself. Most rainmakers will tell you that they like people; that they love to win a client; that it is the thrill of the hunt that energizes them.

Some recognized this at an early age:

"As a Cub Scout, I sold canned nuts door-to-door to raise money for the troop, $1 a can. I learned to like ringing doorbells and finding the surprise inside."

Robert Stein, of counsel, Coblentz Patch Duffy & Bass LLP

For others, it came later:

"I had to be told that I was a rainmaker. I had a misperception that a rainmaker was the best lawyer in the firm. Once I realized that there

> *were many ways to be successful, that I didn't have to learn how to play golf or like sports, and that my people skills were an asset for business development, I have enjoyed this aspect of my work."*
>
> Anne Cappella, partner, Weil, Gotshal & Manges LLP

Are rainmakers born or bred? The answer is both. And regardless of when you have the "aha!" moment that you, too, can be a rainmaker, I am hopeful that this book will provide some practical tips to help you along the way. Because making it rain is here to stay in the legal profession. So, as my good friend Mary Craig Calkins, a partner at Kirkland & Ellis LLP, says: "Just do it".

About Globe Law and Business

Globe Law and Business was established in 2005. From the very beginning, we set out to create law books that are sufficiently high level to be of real use to the experienced professional, yet still accessible and easy to navigate. Most of our authors are drawn from Magic Circle and other top commercial firms, both in the United Kingdom and internationally.

Our titles are carefully produced, with the utmost attention paid to editorial, design and production processes. We hope this results in high-quality publications that are easy to read and a pleasure to own. Our titles are also available as ebooks, which are compatible with most desktop, laptop and tablet devices. In 2018 we expanded our portfolio to include journals and Special Reports, available both digitally and in hard copy format, and produced to the same high standards as our books.

In 2021, we were very pleased to announce the start of a new chapter for Globe Law and Business following the acquisition of law books under the imprint Ark Publishing. Our law firm management list is now significantly expanded with many well known and loved Ark Publishing titles.

We are also pleased to announce the launch of our online content platform, Globe Law Online. This allows for easy search and networked access across firms. Key collections include the Law Firm Management Collection, Private Client and Energy and the Energy Transition. Email me at sian@globelawandbusiness.com for further details or to arrange a free trial for you or your firm.

Sian O'Neill
Managing director
Globe Law and Business
www.globelawandbusiness.com

www.ingramcontent.com/pod-product-compliance
Ingram Content Group UK Ltd.
Pitfield, Milton Keynes, MK11 3LW, UK
UKHW021848150926
8657IPUK00005B/139